I0804183

TO LIVE IN CHRIST

What *it* Means *to be* Christian

TO LIVE IN CHRIST

What it Means *to be* Christian

RODOLFO VALDÉS (ED.)

Scepter

This is a translation and adaptation of articles from opusdei.org entitled *Para mí, vivir es Cristo: Coordenadas para una vida centrada en Jesucristo,* copyright © 2021 Opus Dei information office.

Published by Scepter Publishers, Inc.
info@scepterpublishers.org
www.scepterpublishers.org
800-322-8773
New York

Cover Design by Alston Taggart and Kevin Sample at StudioRed Design
Text by PerfecType, Nashville, TN
Cover Image by Mark Tegethoff on Unsplash

Library of Congress Control Number: 2021945386

Paperback: 9781594174346
eBook: 9781594174353

Printed in the United States of America

CONTENTS

Foreword

Rodolfo Valdés

WHAT DOES IT MEAN to be a Christian? There are many ways to answer this question. Perhaps one of the most succinct is the one found several times in the letters of St. Paul: to be a Christian is to live in Christ, to live our life with him, to live his life in ours. In him God chose us "before the foundation of the world, that we should be holy" (Eph 1:4); in him we are baptized to share in his death and resurrection (see Rom 6:1–14); in him we become a "new creation" (2 Cor 5:17).

Life in Christ leads us to go beyond the limits of a self-enclosed existence. It opens us to the horizon of communion with God and with the people around us, leaving behind the dissatisfaction brought about by exclusively worldly concerns. It gives us a new hope, which acts in our daily life and, at the same time, projects itself beyond death: "None of us lives to himself, and none of us dies to himself. If we live, we live to the Lord, and if we die, we die to the Lord; so then, whether we live or whether we die, we are the Lord's" (Rom 14:7–8). Life in Christ is a gift that we receive in a particular way by participating in the sacraments, and which translates into an existence guided by the Holy Spirit, marked by Love (see Rom 8).

The Person of Jesus Christ must therefore be the starting point and the guiding thread of our whole existence. In one of his first pastoral letters, the Prelate of Opus Dei, Msgr. Fernando Ocáriz, recalled this basic principle of Christian life, and pointed out some of its many consequences.

Putting Jesus at the center of our life means deepening in our contemplative prayer in the middle of the world and helping others to travel along "paths of contemplation." It means rediscovering with new light the anthropological and Christian value of the various ascetical means; reaching the person in all of his or her integrity: intellect, will, heart, relations with others; fostering interior freedom, which leads us to do things for love; helping people to think, so that each person can discover what God is asking of them and make decisions with full personal responsibility; nourishing confidence in God's grace, in order to be on the alert against voluntarism and sentimentalism; expressing the ideal of Christian life without confusing it with perfectionism, and teaching people how to live with and accept their own weakness and that of others; practicing, with all its consequences, a daily attitude of hopeful abandonment to God's will, grounded on divine filiation.

In this way the sense of mission that our vocation entails will be strengthened along with our complete and joyful self-giving. We are called to contribute, with initiative and spontaneity, to improving the world and the culture of our times, so that God's plans for mankind are opened: *cogitationes cordis eius,* the plans of his heart which are sustained from generation to generation (see Ps 33:11).[1]

The following paragraphs of the same letter add other aspects that derive from the centrality of Jesus Christ in our life, such as the need to have a heart detached from material goods, so that we are truly "free to love," and our love for the Church, which "will spur us to obtain resources for the development of the apostolates, and to foster in everyone a great professional eagerness."[2] It also considers the sense of mission of those who know they are called by a "God who is love and puts love into us so that we can love him and love others."[3] After all, at times the world seems too small and the time too short to share the gift we have received.

---

1. Fernando Ocáriz, Pastoral Letter, February 14, 2017, no.8. The Prelate, Pastoral Messages. Opus Dei website: www.opusdei.org.
2. Fernando Ocáriz, Pastoral Letter, February 14, 2017, no.8.
3. Fernando Ocáriz, Pastoral Letter, February 14, 2017, no.9.

Contemplative prayer in the world, which Msgr. Ocáriz describes as the first of the consequences of this centrality of Christ in the life of believers, was covered in the book *Divine Insights*. Since then, various authors have written articles that explore other aspects in greater depth. These texts, also published on the Opus Dei website,[4] are now offered in this book, in order to facilitate their reading and to appreciate their thematic connection. Beginning with the centrality of the Person of Jesus as the source of a joy full of hope, they then deal with: the life of prayer in the midst of the world, from a more comprehensive perspective; Christian formation as a process that reaches the person in all its dimensions; the interior freedom of the children of God; the spiritual struggle as a grateful response to God's gift to us in Christ; the sense of mission characteristic of those who have accepted a divine call; and the awareness of the Lord's unconditional love as the foundation of our efforts to please him.

Certainly, there are many issues that remain to be addressed, and even those addressed here could be the subject of further articles. We have not, however, attempted to exhaust a subject which is so wide. On the other hand, it is our hope that the texts collected here will be an invitation to our readers to enter ever more deeply into the mystery of a God who comes to meet us, so that we can all say with St. Paul: "For to me to live is Christ" (Phil 1:21).

---

4. https://opusdei.org/en-us/article/free-ebook-for-me-to-live-is-christ/

ONE

In the Joyful Hope of Christ

Lucas Buch

WHAT GIVES LIFE ITS value? What gives *my* life its value? In today's world the answer to these questions often hinges on two points: the success I can achieve, and the opinions other people have of me. These points are far from negligible. It is only natural to hope our efforts will be successful, as nobody starts something with the aim of failing; and other people's opinions affect our families, social lives, and professional lives. However, in life there are always failures, small or not so small, and it can happen that people form an opinion of us which we simply do not recognize as true.

The experience of failure, loss of standing, or awareness of our own inability—not just in professional life, but even in the effort to live a Christian life—can lead to discouragement, dejection, and ultimately a loss of hope. The pressure to succeed at different levels, *to be someone*, or at least to be able to claim to be someone, is stronger today than ever before. Indeed, more than what one is (a son or daughter, a parent, a brother or sister, a grandparent), the focus nowadays is on what one can *do*. Consequently, people are more vulnerable to the different types of failure that life can bring. Setbacks that before were either resolved or accepted with fortitude, now can often be the cause of deep distress or frustration, even from a very young age. In a world with such high expectations and disillusionments, is it still possible to live "rejoicing in your hope" as St. Paul advises (Rom 12:12)?

In his February 2017 letter, the Prelate of Opus Dei pointed to the only truly enlightening answer to this question, voiced with a decisive "yes!": "Grant, O Lord, that from faith in your Love, we may live each day with a love that is always new, in joyful hope."[1] Even though we may

1. Fernando Ocáriz, Pastoral Letter, February 14, 2017.

sometimes be tempted to lose hope, to do so would mean closing our eyes to God's love and his constant closeness. As Pope Francis reminded us in his catechesis about hope:

> Christian hope is steadfast; that is why it does not disappoint. . . . It is not based on what we can do or be, nor even on what we may believe in. Its foundation, that is, the foundation of Christian hope, is what we can believe most firmly and be most certain of, that is to say, the love that God himself has for each of us. It is easy to say 'God loves us.' We all say it. But think a bit: is each one of us able to say, 'I am sure that God loves *me*'? It is not so easy to say it. But it is true.[2]

The Great Hope

In his preaching and conversations, St. Josemaría often pointed to the first Christians. For them the faith was more than a doctrine to accept or a model of how to live; it was the *gift* of a new life: the gift of the Holy Spirit, who had been poured out into their hearts after Christ's resurrection. For the early Christians, faith in God was a reality they experienced and not simply an intellectual conviction. God was someone really present in their heart. St. Paul wrote to the

---

2. Pope Francis, General Audience (February 15, 2017). Vatican website: www.vatican.va.

faithful at Ephesus, referring to their life before they knew the Gospel: "Remember that you were at that time separated from Christ . . . strangers to the covenants of promise, having no hope and without God in the world" (Eph 2:12). With faith, in contrast, they received hope, "and hope does not disappoint us, because God's love has been poured into our hearts through the Holy Spirit who has been given to us" (Rom 5:5).

Two thousand years later, God continues calling us to this "great hope," which makes all other hopes and disappointments merely relative. "We need the greater and lesser hopes that keep us going day by day. But these are not enough without the great hope, which must surpass everything else. This great hope can only be God, who encompasses the whole of reality and who can bestow upon us what we, by ourselves, cannot attain."[3]

It is good to ask ourselves whether we have become "accustomed" to the reality of a God who saves, a God who comes to fill us with hope; so accustomed that we sometimes fail to see in it anything more than an idea with little real impact on our life. The Cross, which seemed a great failure to those who had hoped in Jesus, became at the Resurrection the most decisive triumph in all history. Decisive because it was a success not limited to Jesus only; we are all

3. Benedict XVI, Encyclical on Christian Hope *Spe Salvi* (November 30, 2007), 31. Vatican website: www.vatican.va.

victors in him. "This is the victory that overcomes the world; our faith" in the Risen One (1 Jn 5:4). The disciples on the road to Emmaus looked at the past with nostalgia: "we had hoped . . ." (Lk 24:21). They did not realize that Jesus was walking with them, that he was about to open their eyes to a wonderful future, proof against any disillusionment. *Stir up the fire of your faith! Christ is not a figure of the past. He is not a memory lost in history. He lives! As St. Paul says,* Iesus Christus heri et hodie: ipse et in saecula! *"Jesus Christ is the same yesterday and today—yes, and forever!"*[4]

Letting Ourselves Be Touched by God's Love

This is how St. Paul summed up our Christian life: "I have been crucified with Christ; it is no longer I who live, but Christ who lives in me; and the life I now live in the flesh I live by faith in the Son of God, who loved me and gave himself for me" (Gal 2:20). For St. Paul, Christianity primarily means that Christ has died for us, has risen, and from heaven has sent into our hearts his Holy Spirit, who transforms us and opens our eyes to a new life. "Whoever is moved by love begins to perceive what 'life' really is. He begins to perceive the meaning of the word hope."[5] As with the Samaritan woman, Mary Magdalene, Nicodemus,

4. St. Josemaría, *The Way* (Princeton, NJ: Scepter, 2001), 584.
5. Benedict XVI, *Spe Salvi*, 27.

Dimas the good thief, and the disciples at Emmaus, Jesus gives us a new way of looking at the world: at ourselves, at others, and at God. And it is only with this new way of looking given to us by God that our struggle to improve and to imitate him makes sense. Otherwise, all our efforts are "vanity and a striving after wind" (Eccl 2:11).

By dying on the cross "for us men and our salvation,"[6] Christ freed us from a relationship with God based on negative precepts and limits and brought us instead a life of love. "You have . . . put on the new nature, which is being renewed in knowledge after the image of its creator" (Col 3:9–10). It means therefore *coming to know* God's love and *letting oneself be touched* by him, in order to set out afresh on the path to holiness.

Finding God and letting ourselves be transformed by him is the key. The Prelate of Opus Dei reminded us of this shortly after his election:

> What are the priorities that our Lord is presenting to us at this historical moment of the world, the Church and the Work? The answer is clear: in the first place, to care for our union with God with the refinement of people in love, beginning with the contemplation of Jesus Christ, the face of the Father's Mercy. The program described by St. Josemaría is always valid:

6. Nicene Creed, in *The Roman Missal.*

> *May you seek Christ, may you find Christ, may you love Christ.*[7]

Union with God enables us to live the life that he offers us. Seeking Christ's face and letting ourselves be looked at by him is a marvelous way to deepen in this life of love.

Letting Ourselves Be Looked at by Christ

Christ is the *face* of God's mercy because in him God talks to us in a language adapted to our level. It is a human language that seeks to satisfy the thirst for love beyond measure that he himself has placed in each one of us. "And you . . . ," Pope Francis asks,

> have you sometimes felt this gaze on you, a gaze of infinite love that, beyond all your sins, limitations and failures, continues to trust you and to look at your life with hope? Are you aware of the value you have for God, who for love has given you everything? As St. Paul teaches us, "God proves his love for us in that while we still were sinners, Christ died for us" (Rom 5:8). Do we really understand the force of these words?[8]

7. Fernando Ocáriz, Pastoral Letter, February 14, 2017, no. 30 (see St. Josemaría, *The Way*, 382).

8. Pope Francis, Message for the Thirty-First World Youth Day (August 15, 2015). Vatican website: www.vatican.va.

To discover our Lord's face, we need to follow the path of adoration and contemplation. "How good it is to be before a crucifix, or on our knees before the Blessed Sacrament, and simply to be in his Presence. How much good it does us when he once more touches our lives and impels us to share his new life!"[9] As the Pope said on one occasion, it means "looking at the face of God, but above all realizing that he is also looking at us."[10] It might seem easy *to let oneself be looked at*, simply *to be* in God's presence. But in this hyperactive world of ours saturated with stimuli, it can be quite a challenge. So we need to ask God for the gift of being able to enter his silence and let ourselves be looked at by him. We need to be convinced that to be in his presence is already a wonderful prayer and tremendously effective, even though we make no immediate resolution. Contemplating Christ's face has a transforming power that we cannot measure with our human criteria. "I keep the Lord always before me; because he is at my right hand, I shall not be moved. Therefore my heart is glad, and my soul rejoices; my body also dwells secure" (Ps 16:8–9).

Jesus' face is also the face of the Crucified. On confronting our own weakness, we could think with overly

---

9. Pope Francis, Apostolic Exhortation on the Proclamation of the Gospel in Today's World *Evangelii Gaudium* (November 24, 2013), 264. Vatican website: www.vatican.va.

10. Pope Francis, Address on the Vigil of Pentecost with the Ecclesial Movements (May 18, 2013). Vatican website: www.vatican.va.

human reasoning that we have let him down, and that we cannot just approach him as though nothing had happened. But these qualms come from a false idea of God's love.

> *There is a false asceticism which presents our Lord on the Cross as furious and rebellious. A contorted body apparently threatening mankind: "You have broken me, but I will hurl down on you my nails, my cross and my thorns!" Such people do not know the spirit of Christ. He suffered all that He could—and being God, how much He could suffer! But He was loving even more than He was suffering. . . . And after dying, He consented to let the lance open another wound, so that you and I might find refuge next to his most loving Heart.*[11]

How well our Father understood the love radiating from Jesus' face! From the cross he looks at us and says, "I know you perfectly. Before dying I could see all your weaknesses and failings, all your falls and betrayals. And knowing you so well, just as you are, *I judged it worthwhile to give my life for you.*" Christ looks at us with a loving, affirmative look. He sees the good in us—the good that *we are* and that he himself has given us on calling us into existence. A good that is worthy of love, of the greatest Love (see Jn 3:16; 15:13).

---

11. St. Josemaría, *The Way of the Cross* (New York: Scepter, 1990), Twelfth Station, no. 3.

Walking with Christ, Leaving a Mark on the World

Jesus' look will help us react with hope when we are faced with our own falls, mistakes, and mediocrity. It is not just about being good ourselves. God is counting on us to change the world and fill it with his love. This call is also contained in Christ's loving look.

> You might say to me, "Father, but I have my limits, I am a sinner, what can I do?" When the Lord calls us, he doesn't worry about what we are, what we have been, or what we have done or not done. Quite the opposite. When he calls us, he is thinking about everything we must give, all the love we can spread. His bets are on the future, on tomorrow. Jesus is pointing you towards the future, never to the museum.[12]

Our Lord's look is a look of love that always *affirms* the person and says, "How good it is that you exist! How wonderful to have you here with me!"[13] At the same time, while knowing us perfectly, *he counts on us*. To discover God's affirming look is the best way to recover our hope

---

12. Pope Francis, Address at the Prayer Vigil with Young People (July 30, 2016). Vatican website: www.vatican.va.

13. See Josef Pieper, *Faith. Hope. Love* (San Francisco: Ignatius Press, 1997), cited by Benedict XVI in Address on the Occasion of Christmas Greetings to the Roman Curia (December 22, 2011). Vatican website: www.vatican.va.

and once again feel drawn upwards, towards love, and then to bring this love to the whole world. Here is our firmest security: Christ died for me because he saw it worthwhile to do so. Christ, who really knows me, has confidence in me. As the Apostle exclaimed: "If God is for us, who is against us? He who did not spare his own Son but gave him up for us all, will he not also give us all things with him?" (Rom 8: 31–32).

This certainty spurs us to set out once again, to launch out again into the whole world to leave on it Christ's mark. We know that we will often stumble, that we will not always achieve what we set out to do, but in the end that is not what really matters. What matters is that we go forward, with our eyes set on our Lord: *expectantes beatam spem,* waiting in joyful hope.[14] It is he who saves us and relies on us to fill the world with peace and joy. "God has created us to be on our feet. There is a lovely song that mountain climbers sing as they climb. It goes like this: 'In climbing it doesn't matter if we stumble and fall, as long as we get up again.'"[15] On our feet, cheerful, confident, going forward with the mission of lighting up *all the ways of the earth with the fire of Christ that you carry in your heart.*[16]

---

14. Communion Rite, in *The Roman Missal.*

15. Pope Francis, Homily, Jubilee for Boys and Girls (April 24, 2016). Vatican website: www.vatican.va.

16. St. Josemaría, *The Way*, 1.

TWO

Paths of Contemplation

Juan Francisco Pozo and Rodolfo Valdés

ONE OF THE ATTITUDES the Gospels highlight about Jesus' fulfillment of his mission is how often he has recourse to prayer. The rhythm of his ministry is marked by the times when he turns to the Father. Jesus prays before his baptism (see Lk 3:21), the night before choosing the twelve (see Lk 6:12), on the mountain before the Transfiguration (see Lk 9:28), and in the Garden of Olives while preparing to face his passion (see Lk 22:41–44). Our Lord spent a lot of time in prayer: at dusk, or the whole night, or very early in the morning, or amid days of intense preaching. In fact, he prayed constantly, and repeatedly reminded his disciples of the need to "pray always without becoming weary" (Lk 18:1, NABRE).

Why this example and insistence by our Lord? Why is prayer so necessary? Prayer responds to the most intimate desires of each human being, created to enter into dialogue with God and contemplate him. But prayer, above all, is a gift from God, a gift that he offers to us: "The living and true God tirelessly calls each person to that mysterious encounter known as prayer. In prayer, the faithful God's initiative of love always comes first; our own first step is always a response."[1]

To imitate Christ and share in his life, we must be souls of prayer. Through the contemplation of the mystery of God, revealed in Jesus Christ, our life is gradually transformed into his. St. Paul's words to the Corinthians become a reality: "And we all, with unveiled face, beholding the glory of the Lord, are being changed into his likeness from one degree of glory to another; for this comes from the Lord who is the Spirit" (2 Cor 3:18). Like St. Paul, all Christians are called to reflect Christ's face in their own features: by being apostles, messengers of God's love, which

---

1. *Catechism of the Catholic Church,* 2nd ed. (Washington, DC: Libreria Editrice Vaticana–United States Conference of Catholic Bishops, 2000), 2567.

is experienced personally during times of prayer. That is why we need to "deepen in our contemplative prayer in the middle of the world, and help others to travel along *paths of contemplation*."[2]

Accepting God's Gift

An apostle grows at the rhythm of prayer, and contemplation is the starting point for growing in the eagerness to evangelize. As the Pope reminds us: "The best incentive for sharing the Gospel comes from contemplating it with love, lingering over its pages and reading it with the heart. If we approach it in this way, its beauty will amaze and constantly excite us."[3] Therefore we need to acquire "a contemplative spirit which can help us to realize ever anew that we have been entrusted with a treasure which makes us more human and helps us to lead a new life. There is nothing more precious which we can give to others."[4]

The Gospels introduce us to a variety of persons whose encounter with Christ changes their life and makes them the bearers of our Lord's saving message. One of these is the Samaritan woman who, as St. John recounts, only wants to fetch water at the well where Jesus is sitting and resting. It is

---

2. Fernando Ocáriz, Pastoral Letter, February 14, 2017, 8. Quoting St. Josemaría, *Friends of God* (London: Scepter, 1981), 67.

3. Pope Francis, *Evangelii Gaudium*, 264.

4. Pope Francis, *Evangelii Gaudium,* 264.

he who begins the dialogue: "Give me a drink" (Jn 4:7). At first, the Samaritan woman is not very willing to continue the conversation: "How is it that you, a Jew, ask a drink of me, a woman of Samar'ia?" (Jn 4:9). But our Lord makes her see that he is the water she is seeking: "If you knew the gift of God . . ." (Jn 4:10); "whoever drinks of the water that I shall give him will never thirst; the water that I shall give him will become in him a spring of water welling up to eternal life" (Jn 4:14).

After reaching the Samaritan woman's heart, Christ reveals with clarity and simplicity that he knows her past (see 4:17–18). But he does so with such great love that she does not feel discouraged or rejected. On the contrary, Jesus introduces her to a new universe, a new world of hope, because the moment of reconciliation has arrived, the moment when the doors of prayer are opened to all men and women: "Woman, believe me, the hour is coming when neither on this mountain nor in Jerusalem will you worship the Father. . . . The hour is coming, and now is, when the true worshipers will worship the Father in spirit and truth (Jn 4:21, 23).

In her dialogue with Jesus, the Samaritan woman discovers the truth about God and about her own life. She accepts God's gift and is radically converted. Therefore, the Church has seen in this Gospel passage one of the most expressive images of prayer: "Jesus thirsts; his asking arises from the depths of God's desire for us. Whether we realize it or not, prayer is the encounter of God's thirst with ours. God thirsts that we may thirst for him."[5]

Prayer is a sign of God's initiative, who goes out in search of us and waits for our response to make us his friends. Sometimes it can seem that we are the ones who take the initiative to dedicate time to prayer, but in reality, it is a response to God's call. Prayer is in truth a reciprocal call: God seeks me and waits for me, and I need God and seek him.

Time for God

Men and women thirst for God, even though they often fail to realize it, and even refuse to go to the sources of living water, which are the times dedicated to prayer. The story of the Samaritan woman is repeated in many souls. Jesus asks for a little attention and tries to begin a dialogue in a person's heart, at a moment that perhaps seems untimely.

Devoting time to our Lord is not just one more job on a to-do list or another burden on an already demanding schedule. It is rather the acceptance of an infinitely valuable gift, a precious pearl or hidden treasure amid our normal daily life that we need to care for lovingly.

---

5. *Catechism of the Catholic Church*, 2560 (referencing St. Augustine, *De diversis quaestionibus octoginta tribus* 64,4:PL 40, 56).

The choice of when to pray depends on a will that wants to be conquered by love; prayer isn't done when we have extra time, but rather we need to make time for prayer. When prayer is left for the gaps that may appear in a person's daily schedule, it will likely not be done regularly. The choice of when to devote time to prayer reveals the secrets of a person's heart; it shows the place that love for God occupies in the hierarchy of our daily interests.[6]

Prayer is always possible. A Christian's time belongs to the risen Christ, who is with us every day (see Mt 28:20). The most frequent temptation for setting aside prayer is a certain lack of faith, which shows our true preferences: "When we begin to pray, a thousand labors or cares thought to be urgent vie for priority; once again, it is the moment of truth for the heart: what is its real love?"[7] Our Lord comes first. Therefore, we need to decide on the best time for prayer, perhaps seeking advice in spiritual direction, in order to adapt that plan to our personal circumstances.

St. Josemaría often prayed in the car during his apostolic trips; he also prayed on the tram, or walking through the streets of Madrid, when he had no other opportunities. Those who are striving for sanctity in the middle of ordinary life can find themselves in similar situations; a father or a mother may sometimes have no other option but to pray

6. See *Catechism of the Catholic Church*, 2710.
7. See *Catechism of the Catholic Church*, 2732.

while caring for their little children. This is very pleasing to God. But realizing that our Lord is waiting for us and wants to offer us the graces we need in our prayer can encourage us to choose the best possible time and place for it.

Spiritual Combat in Prayer

To consider prayer as an art implies recognizing that we can always grow in its practice, allowing God's grace to act ever more fully in our souls. Hence prayer is also combat.[8] It is a struggle, first, against ourselves. Distractions invade the mind when we try to create inner silence. They reveal to us what our heart is attached to and can serve as a light to ask God for help.[9]

Today we have abundant technological possibilities that facilitate communication in many ways but that also increase occasions for distraction. Hence we are facing a new challenge for growing in our contemplative life: learning to foster inner silence while surrounded by so much external noise. But in the face of this situation, new importance is also being given today to values such as attention and concentration, seen as a way to protect our capacity to pause and inquire into what is truly worthwhile.

---

8. See *Catechism of the Catholic Church*, 2725 and ff.
9. See *Catechism of the Catholic Church*, 2729.

Interior silence is a necessary condition for the contemplative life. It frees us from the attachment to the immediate, to what seems easy, to what distracts but does not fulfill us, so that we can focus on our true good: on our Lord Jesus Christ, who comes to meet us in prayer.

Interior recollection involves moving away from being dispersed in many activities and toward a stronger interior world. There it is easier for us to find God and recognize his presence in our daily lives, in small signs of his action each day, in lights we receive, or in the attitudes of other people. And thus, we are better able to express to him our adoration, repentance, thanksgiving, and petition. That is why interior recollection is so vital for a contemplative soul in the middle of the world. *True prayer that absorbs a person's whole life is fostered—more than by the solitude of the desert—by interior recollection.*[10]

In Search of New Lights

If you put your mind to it, everything in your life can be offered to God and provide an opportunity to talk with your Father in Heaven, who always wants to grant you new lights.[11] Certainly God, in granting these lights, counts on our ardent search for him, we who are ready to listen with simplicity

10. St. Josemaría, *Furrow* (New York: Scepter, 1987), 460.
11. St. Josemaría, *The Forge* (New York: Scepter, 1987), 743.

to the word he addresses to us and set aside the thought that there is nothing new to discover there. Here the attitude of the Samaritan woman at the well is an example for us, since she kept alive in her heart the desire for the Messiah's arrival.

This effort will lead us to bring the happenings of each day to our dialogue with our Lord, but without expecting an immediate solution that suits our pressing needs. It is more important to consider what our Lord wants from us, since more often than not, the only thing he expects of us is to put ourselves with simplicity before him and gratefully recall all that the Holy Spirit is doing silently within us. Or it may also involve taking scenes from the Gospels and calmly contemplating them and taking part as *another character*,[12] letting ourselves be challenged by Christ.

When Words Don't Come

Nevertheless, despite our efforts, we can sometimes encounter difficulties in our dialogue with God. How comforting it is then to remember our Lord's admonition: "In praying do not heap up empty phrases as the Gentiles do; for they think that they will be heard for their many words" (Mt 6:7). It is time once again to trust in the action of the Holy Spirit, who "helps us in our weakness; for we do not

---

12. St. Josemaría, *Friends of God*, 222.

know how to pray as we ought, but the Spirit himself intercedes for us with sighs too deep for words" (Rom 8:26).

Commenting on these words of St. Paul, Benedict XVI described the attitude of abandonment that should imbue our prayer:

> We want to pray, but God is far, we do not have the words, the language, to speak with God, not even the thought. We can only open ourselves, set our time at the disposal of God, waiting for him to help us enter true dialogue. The Apostle says: this very lack of words, this absence of words, even the desire to enter into contact with God is a prayer that the Holy Spirit not only understands, but carries, interprets, to God. It is precisely our weakness which becomes, through the Holy Spirit, true prayer, true contact with God.[13]

Therefore, we shouldn't become discouraged if we find it difficult to keep up a dialogue with our Lord. When our heart seems closed to spiritual realities, when the minutes spent in prayer become long and our thoughts wander to other things, perhaps the following considerations from St. Josemaría can help us:

> *Remember that prayer does not consist in making pretty speeches, or high-sounding or consoling phrases.*

---

13. Benedict XVI, General Audience (May 16), 2012. Vatican website: www.vatican.va.

Prayer, at times, will be a glance at a picture of our Lord or of his Mother; sometimes a petition, expressed in words; or offering good works, and the fruits of faithfulness.

We have to be like a guard on sentry duty at the gate of God our Lord: that's what prayer is. Or like a small dog that lies down at its master's feet.

Don't mind telling him: Lord, here I am, like a faithful dog; or better still like a little donkey, who won't kick the one who loves him.[14]

The Source That Changes the World

True prayer is impactful: it affects our life, illuminates it, and opens our eyes to our surroundings with a supernatural perspective. As Pope St. John Paul II said: "Intense prayer . . . does not distract us from our commitment to history: by opening our heart to the love of God it also opens it to the love of our brothers and sisters, and makes us capable of shaping history according to God's plan."[15]

In prayer, our Lord not only wants to quench our thirst but also to encourage us to share with others the joy of drawing close to him. This is what happened in the

14. St. Josemaría, *The Forge*, 73.

15. Pope St. John Paul II, Apostolic Letter at the Close of the Great Jubilee Year 2000 *Novo Millennio Ineunte* (January 6, 2001), 33. Vatican website: www.vatican.va.

heart of the Samaritan woman. After her encounter with Jesus, she hastens to make him known to those around her. "Many Samaritans from that city believed in him because of the woman's testimony, 'He told me all that I ever did'" (Jn 4:39). A sign of authentic prayer is the desire to share the experience of Christ with others: "What kind of love would not feel the need to speak of the beloved, to point him out, to make him known?"[16]

Our holy mother Mary teaches us how to pray. Our Lady meditated in her heart on the concerns of her Son (see Lk 2:51) and accompanied Jesus' disciples in prayer (see Acts 1:14). She showed them the path for receiving, in all its fullness, the gift of the Holy Spirit, who will spur them to launch out in the divine adventure of evangelization.

16. Pope Francis, *Evangelii Gaudium*, no. 264.

THREE

Reaching the Entire Person: The Role of the Emotions

Julio Diéguez

CERTAINLY, JESUS CHRIST IS the love of our life: not the greatest among others, but the one who gives meaning to all our other loves, and to the interests, dreams, ambitions, jobs, and initiatives that fill our days and our hearts. Hence in our spiritual life we need to preserve the centrality of the

Person of Jesus Christ.[1] He is the path to enter into communion with the Father in the Holy Spirit. In him is revealed the mystery of "who man is"[2] and what we are called to. To walk with Christ means to grow in self-knowledge and to enter more deeply into our own personal mystery. To allow Jesus to be the center of our life leads, among other things, to rediscovering with new light the anthropological and Christian value of the various ascetical means; reaching the person in all his or her integrity: intellect, will, heart, and relations with others.[3]

The person we must reach first is our own self, and then all those with whom we come in contact through our friendship and apostolate. The formation that we receive and that we impart should reach the intellect, the will, and the emotions, with none of these elements being neglected or simply "subordinated" to the others. Here we will concentrate primarily on forming each person's emotional life, taking as given the need for solid intellectual formation as the foundation. The consideration of the importance of integral formation will allow us to "rediscover" the great truth contained in St. Josemaría's identification of "fidelity" with "happiness."[4]

---

1. Fernando Ocáriz, Pastoral Letter, February 14, 2017, 8.

2. See Second Vatican Council, Pastoral Constitution on the Church in the Modern World *Gaudium et Spes* (December 7, 1965), 22. Vatican website: www.vatican.va.

3. Fernando Ocáriz, Pastoral Letter, February 14, 2017, 8.

4. In Spanish: "fidelidad" and "felicidad." See St. Josemaría, *Furrow*, 84: "Your steadfastness in faith, purity and the way God has

Being Formed in Accord with Christ's Heart

Some people, when they think of formation, tend to consider it as knowledge. Thus, a person who has received good doctrinal, ascetical, and professional information is considered to have good formation. But more than that is required. To reach the person in all his or her integrity requires viewing formation as a way of being. Good professionals know the body of information and techniques required by their profession, but they have acquired something else as well. They have developed habits—ways of being—that enable them to apply that knowledge and those techniques successfully: habits of attention to others, concentration in work, punctuality, coping with successes and failures, perseverance, and so on.

Similarly, being a good Christian doesn't simply mean knowing (at a level appropriate to one's situation in the Church and in society) the Church's teaching on the sacraments or on prayer, or on general and professional moral norms. The goal is much higher: immersing ourselves in the mystery of Christ so as to grasp it in all its breadth and depth (see Eph 3:18), letting his life enter ours, and being able to say with St. Paul, "it is no longer I who live, but Christ who lives in me" (Gal 2:20). Thus, it means being "*alter Christus,*

---

marked out for you is the measure of your happiness on earth." See also, for example, Instruction, May1935/September 14, 1950, 60; Instruction December 8, 1941, 61; St. Josemaría, *Friends of God*, 189.

ipse Christus" (another Christ, Christ himself),[5] allowing grace to transform us gradually so as to configure us to him.

Letting grace act is not something merely passive; it doesn't mean simply not placing obstacles in the way, since the Holy Spirit doesn't transform us into Christ without our free, voluntary cooperation. But neither is that enough. To give ourselves to our Lord, to give him our life, is not simply to give him our decisions, and our actions; it is also to give him our hearts, our feelings, our spontaneity. To do so, we need to have a good intellectual and doctrinal formation that shapes our minds and influences our decisions, but this doctrine also must sink in deeply and reach our hearts. And this requires struggle; it requires time. In other words, it requires acquiring virtues, which is precisely what formation consists of.

It is not uncommon to meet people who fear that insisting on the virtues may end up leading to "voluntarism," to giving primacy to a person's willpower. Nothing could be further from the truth. Perhaps at the root of that confusion is an erroneous idea of virtue, which is seen as simply a supplement to willpower, enabling the person who possesses it to fulfill the moral law even when it goes against their own inclination. This is quite a widespread idea and does in fact stem from voluntarism. Virtue is thus regarded as

5. St. Josemaría, *Christ is Passing By* (New York: Scepter, 1974), 96.

the capacity to go against the flow of our own inclinations when the moral law so requires.

There is of course some truth in this. But it is an incomplete vision, in which virtues are turned into cold qualities that would lead to rejecting in practice our own inclinations, interests, and affections, and that would inevitably result in turning indifference into an ideal—as though the interior life and self-giving consisted in reaching the point where we don't feel attracted by anything that might influence our own future decisions.

To regard formation in that way would make it impossible to reach person in their integrity. The intellect, will, and emotions would not be growing together, helping one another to advance. Rather one of these faculties would dominate and stifle the others. The correct development of the interior life, in contrast, requires integration, and certainly doesn't lead to a diminishing or loss of our interests and emotions. Quite the opposite. The interior life expands the heart and fills it with a great love, enabling us to view our emotions in a broader context that provides the means for tackling feelings that give rise to difficulties, and helps capture the positive and transcendent meaning of those that are pleasant.

The Gospels show us our Lord's sincere concern for his disciples' rest. "And he said to them, 'Come away by yourselves to a lonely place, and rest a while'" (Mk 6:31). We also see how his heart reacts when confronted by his friends' suffering, like Martha's and Mary's (see Jn 11:1–44). We cannot suppose that in those moments Jesus was simply "acting," as though deep down, because of his union with his Father, whatever happened around him was a matter of indifference to him. St. Josemaría often spoke about loving the world passionately.[6] He encouraged people to place their heart in God and, through him, in others, in the work we are engaged in, in our efforts in the apostolate. *Our Lord does not want us to be dry and rigid, like inert matter.*[7]

Availability, for example, is not the disposition of a person who is indifferent to doing this or that because he has succeeded in losing interest in everything, perhaps in order to avoid suffering when something is asked of him which he doesn't like. Rather it is the noble disposition of one who is able at a particular moment to do without something that is good and attractive, in order to concentrate on something else in which God is awaiting us, because living for God is our deepest desire. Such a person has a great heart, filled with interests and good ambitions that can be set aside whenever necessary, not because we reject them or try to avoid being affected by them, but because our interest in loving and serving God is much greater still. And not only

---

6. Suffice it to mention, by way of example, the title of the homily "Passionately Loving the World," in *Conversations with Monsignor Escrivá de Balaguer* (Sydney: Little Hills and Scepter, 1993), 113–123.

7. St. Josemaría, *Friends of God*, 183.

is it greater, but it is, in fact, transformed into what gives meaning to, and what embraces, all other interests.

Rejoicing in Practicing the Virtues

Formation in the virtues requires struggle, overcoming our own inclination when this is opposed to good acts. This is the part of truth that is contained in the reductionist, "voluntaristic" concept of virtue referred to earlier. However virtue doesn't consist in the capacity to oppose inclinations, but rather than in the formation of our inclinations. The goal, then, is not that we should be capable of habitually setting our feelings aside to let ourselves be guided by an external rule, but rather to form those feelings in such a way that we are capable of rejoicing in the good achieved. Virtue consists precisely in this rejoicing in the good, in the formation, we might say, of "good taste": "[Blessed is the man whose] delight is in the law of the Lord, and on his law he meditates day and night" (Ps 1:2). Thus, virtue entails the formation of our feelings, and not the habit of systematically opposing them.

As long as virtue is unformed, our feelings and emotions can resist a good act, resistance which needs to be overcome. But the aim is not simply to overcome the resistance but rather to develop a "taste" for acting virtuously. When one possesses virtue, the good act may still be difficult, but it is performed with joy. For example, to get up on time in the morning—*the heroic minute*[8]—will probably always be difficult; perhaps the day will never come when we don't feel inclined to spend more time in bed. But if we habitually strive to overcome laziness out of love for God, a moment comes when to do so brings us joy, while to give in to comfort displeases us and leaves a bad taste in our mouth.

Forming virtues makes the faculties and affections learn to focus on what truly satisfies our deepest aspirations, while attributing secondary importance—always subordinate to what is most important—to those things that are simply means to an end. In the final analysis, to be formed in the virtues is to learn how to be happy, to rejoice at, and with, what is truly great; it is, in short, to prepare for heaven.

If being formed means growing in virtues, and the virtues consist in a certain order in our affectivity, in our feelings and emotions, we can conclude that all formation is the formation of affectivity. On reading this, someone may raise the objection that, in our effort to acquire virtues, the aim is operative rather than affective, perhaps even adding that we apply the name of *virtues* precisely to operative habits. This is true. But if the virtues help us to do good, it is because they help us to feel correctly. The human being always moves toward the good.

8. St. Josemaría, *The Way*, 206.

The moral problem is the following question: Why is it that what is not good, or not the ultimate good, appears to us as good, in a specific situation? This is due to the disorder in our tendencies. This disorder leads us to exaggerate the value of the good towards which one of those tendencies is directed. We then consider this thing or situation as more desirable than another (greater) good with which it is in conflict, even though this greater good has more value, as it is in harmony with our overall good.

This love for the truth over other goods that also attract us is precisely what we call *sincerity*. But if the desire to look good is stronger than the attraction of truth, it is easy for the reason to be deceived, and even though it knows that it isn't good, it judges that it is appropriate to lie. Although we know perfectly well that it is wrong to lie, we conclude that in this specific situation it is appropriate to do so.

A well-ordered emotional life helps us do good because it helps us to grasp it as good beforehand. Hence the importance of forming our emotions correctly. How can this be done? Before we attempt to answer this question, it is necessary to make some preliminary observations.

The Will and Our Feelings

We have just stated that a well-ordered affectivity helps us to act well. The reverse is also true: to act well helps us to order our affectivity.

We know from experience (and it is good not to forget it if we want to avoid easily falling into frustration and discouragement) that we cannot directly control our feelings. If we fall prey to discouragement, we cannot resolve the problem simply by deciding to feel happy. The same applies if, at a given moment, we want to feel more daring, or less timid, or if we don't want to feel afraid or ashamed, or attracted to something we judge to be disordered.

In short, a voluntary decision to make our feelings correspond to our desires is not enough. However, the fact that the will doesn't directly control our feelings doesn't mean that it has no influence over them.

In ethics, the control that the will can exercise over feelings is called "political," because it is like that which a ruler has over his subjects; he cannot control them directly, since they are free. But he can take certain measures—for example, reducing taxes—in the hope that these will produce specific results—for example, increased consumption or investment—through the free will of the citizens responding to these incentives. We too can perform certain acts which we hope will give rise to specific feelings. For example, we can stop to consider the good that will be done by an apostolic undertaking for which we are seeking help, as a way of feeling more daring when asking for a donation to help get that undertaking started. We can reflect on our divine filiation in the hope that a professional setback will have less of an impact on us at the level of our feelings.

Much more important, however, is the long-term influence that the will exercises over our affectivity, since this influence is precisely what allows it to give it form. Here we are talking about an influence that comes about even without the person seeking it. It results from the fact that voluntary acts can cause changes not only in the world around us but also and above all within us. These acts help produce a connatural affective affinity with the good that the will seeks. Explaining exactly how this comes about is beyond the scope of this chapter, but here we want to highlight two key points.

Wanting the Good

The first is to note that the good toward which the will inclines—and by which this connatural affinity is produced—can be very different from what is perceived from the outside. Two people who carry out the same assignment can be doing two very different things. One may be totally absorbed in not appearing bad in the eyes of the person who has given him that assignment, while the other really wants to serve. This second person is forming a virtue while the first isn't, since the good sought is ultimately that of not looking bad before someone with authority. It is true that this action can be a better step than simply refusing to do the task. But as long as it isn't followed by a series of further steps, that person would not be growing in virtue no matter how many times the action is repeated. Hence it is very important to rectify, to constantly purify our intentions, in order to little by little embrace the reasons for which doing something is worthwhile, and thus to shape our emotions with them.

We have all experienced—or witnessed others experiencing—the way that limiting ourselves to respecting certain rules easily ends up becoming a burden. The example of the older son in the parable of the Prodigal Son warns us of this danger (see Lk 15:29-30). In contrast, sincerely seeking the good that these rules are meant to foster brings freedom and joy. Ultimately, we could say that we need to shape not so much our *doing* as our *wanting*. Not only what I do is important, but also what I want when I do it.[9] Freedom, thus, is the decisive factor. It is not sufficient to do something; we must want to do it. We must do it *because we want to, which is the most supernatural reason*,[10] because only then are we growing in virtue, that is, learning to enjoy what is truly good. A mere fulfillment that leads to *cumplo y miento*, to fulfilling and lying,[11] doesn't lead to freedom, nor to love and joy. But when

---

9. In reality, from a moral standpoint, *what I do* is precisely *what I want when I do it*. But for our purposes here there is no need to pause to explain why this is so.

10. St. Josemaría, *Christ is Passing By*, 17.

11. See Bl. Álvaro del Portillo, Letter, September 1995, in *Family Letters I*, 8.

we understand why this way of acting is truly great and worthwhile, and let ourselves be guided by these reasons in our actions, then we foster our freedom, and strengthen our love and joy.

Long-Term Formation

The second point to consider is that the struggle takes time. If virtue consisted merely in the capacity to overcome the resistance in our feelings to doing what is right, we could acquire it in a much shorter time. But we know that a virtue has not yet been solidly formed if the good being sought doesn't have a positive echo in our emotions.[12] Hence we need to be patient in our struggle because it may take a long time, even years, to achieve certain worthwhile goals. The difficulty we may experience in pursuing the good during this time shouldn't be interpreted as a failure or as a sign that our struggle is not sincere or decisive enough.

If, for example, we want to overcome our angry reactions, we will begin by making the effort to limit the external manifestations. Perhaps at first it may seem that we are not getting anywhere. But if we persist, the times when we control ourselves—perhaps very few at the beginning—will become more and more frequent, and after some time—perhaps

12. It should be clear from what has been said previously that this doesn't mean that the good requires no effort or, what amounts to the same, that evil no longer holds any attraction.

a long time—we will gain habitual self-control. Still, this is not enough, since our goal is not to repress the external manifestations but to shape our internal reaction, to become gentler and more peaceful. And then this calmer reaction will become engrained in our way of being.

Pope Francis, in explaining his principle that *time is greater than space*,[13] points out that "giving priority to time means being concerned about initiating processes *rather than possessing spaces.*"[14] In the interior life it is worthwhile to start realistic and generous processes. And we need to be ready to wait for them to produce fruit. "This principle enables us to work slowly but surely, without being obsessed with immediate results. It helps us patiently to endure difficult and adverse situations, or inevitable changes in our plans. It invites us to accept the tension between fullness and limitation."[15]

To aim high in our formation, to strive not only to *carry out* good acts, but *to be* good, to have a good heart, will enable us to distinguish a virtuous act from what we might call an act that conforms to a virtue. The latter would be an act that corresponds to a virtue and contributes step by step to attaining it, but that since it does not yet stem from a mature habit, often still requires overcoming feelings that pull in the opposite direction. In contrast, a virtuous act is

13. See *Evangelium Gaudium*, 222–225.
14. See *Evangelium Gaudium*, 223. Italics in the original.
15. See *Evangelium Gaudium*, 223.

one that brings joy in accomplishing the good even when this requires effort. That is the goal.

An integral formation that shapes our emotional reactions is a slow process. Those who seek it won't fall into the naive attempt to submit our feelings to the will, suppressing emotions we don't like or trying to stir up those we want to have. We come to understand that our struggle should be centered rather on the free decisions by which, in striving to fulfill God's will, we respond to these feelings, accepting or rejecting the behavior they suggest to us. For it is these decisions that—indirectly and in the long run—lead to forming the intimate world within us from which these feelings stem.

An Interior World

As we grow in virtue, we not only carry out a good act with greater naturalness and joy, but we also become better able to identify what this good act is. As Pope St. John Paul II explained,

> In order to "prove what is the will of God, what is good and acceptable and perfect" (Rom 12:2), knowledge of God's law in general is certainly necessary, but it is not sufficient. What is essential is a sort of "connaturality" between man and the true good (see St. Thomas Aquinas, *Summa Theologiae*, II-II, q. 45, a. 2). Such a connaturality is rooted in

> and develops through the virtuous attitudes of the individual himself.[16]

This is due in large part to the fact that our emotional response is the first voice we hear when evaluating the suitability of a particular way of acting. Even before our reason considers whether it is right or not to do something pleasurable, we have already sensed its appeal. Virtue, by making the good attractive to our feelings, endows the voice of our affective response with a certain moral evaluation (that is, a reference to the person's overall good) of this act.

In an implicit but clear way, we find this expressed in a very brief point of *The Way*: "Why should you look around you, if you carry 'your world' within you?"[17] St. Josemaría is contrasting looking at the exterior world with a person's interior world. And it is this relationship that determines the value of the external look, which will be seen as appropriate or not according to one's interior world. There is no need then to suppress as inappropriate this external look, since right from the start the interior world—"my world"—rejects it. St. Josemaría is telling us that if our interior world is rich, we will not only avoid what can do us harm, but

16. St. John Paul II, Encyclical *Veritatis Splendor* (August 6, 1993), 64. Vatican website: www.vatican.va. The text referred to is St. Thomas Aquinas' *Summa Theologiae*, II–II, q. 45, a. 2.

17. St. Josemaría, *The Way*, 184.

it won't even be a danger because we will find it repugnant. We will see it not only as bad, but also—and even beforehand—as ugly, unappealing, unfitting, out of place. Of course, it may be attractive in some way, but it is easy to reject that attraction because it destroys the beauty and harmony of our interior world. In contrast, if we don't "carry our world within us," avoiding that exterior look will entail considerable effort.

Realism

All this shows how growth in the virtues makes us ever more realistic in our approach to life. Some people have the idea—normally not expressed—that living according to the virtues implies closing our eyes to reality. And this for a very noble reason, because by acting in this way we turn our back on part of this world hoping for a reward in the next. On the contrary, living as Christ did, imitating his virtues, opens us to the real world and prevents our feelings from deceiving us when evaluating and deciding how to respond to it.

For example, poverty doesn't mean failing to appreciate the value of material goods in light of eternal life. Rather, only a person who lives with detachment truly appreciates material goods in the proper way. They aren't seen as evil, nor are they given an importance they don't have. On the other hand, a person who makes no effort to live with detachment will end up giving them a greater value than what they deserve.

A temperate person knows how to enjoy a good meal, while a person who lacks this virtue will give this pleasure an importance it objectively lacks. Something similar could be said about any other virtue. As Jesus told Nicodemus, "He who does what is true comes to the light" (Jn 3:21).

A "Virtuous" Circle

In the end, guiding our feelings by developing the virtues leads to purifying our sight. It is like taking our glasses and cleaning off the stains that original sin and our personal sins have left on them and that make it difficult for us to see the world as it really is. "Let us say it plainly: the unredeemed state of the world consists precisely in the failure to understand the meaning of creation, in the failure to recognize truth; as a result, the rule of pragmatism is imposed, by which the strong arm of the powerful becomes the god of this world."[18]

A well-ordered affectivity helps our reason to *understand creation, to recognize the truth*, to identify what is truly good for us. Correct judgement on the part of our reason facilitates free choice. The good act that results from this choice helps to "connaturalize" us with the good we seek,

18. Joseph Ratzinger – Benedict XVI, *Jesus of Nazareth*, pt. 2, Holy Week, From the Entrance into Jerusalem to the Resurrection (San Francisco: Ignatius Press, 2011), 7, 3.

and consequently to put order into our emotional responses. This produces an authentic "virtuous circle" that leads us to realize that we are progressively freer, masters of our own acts and hence able to truly give ourselves to God, since only a person who possesses himself can give himself.

Formation is integral only when it reaches all these levels. In other words, there is only true formation when the various faculties that intervene in human acts—reason, will, emotions—are integrated. These faculties shouldn't fight with one another but rather work together. If we fail to properly mold our feelings, that is, if the virtues are understood as only an added force for our will that enables it to override our feelings, the moral norms and the struggle to try to live them will be repressive and will fail to lead to an authentic unity of life. For we would always feel within us powerful forces that try to pull us in the opposite direction and produce instability. We are well-acquainted with this instability, since it is where we start. But we can overcome it little by little, as we guide these forces progressively towards harmony. Then the moment will come when "because I want to," which is the "most supernatural reason," comes to mean "because I like it," "because it attracts me," "because it accords with my way of being," "because it fits with the interior world that I have formed for myself." And ultimately, "because I have learned to make my own the sentiments of Christ Jesus."

Thus, we make progress toward the attractive and exalted goal that St. Paul sets out for us: "Have this mind among yourselves, which was in Christ Jesus" (Phil 2:5). And we realize that thus we are putting on the Lord Jesus Christ (see Rom 13:14). *Christ's life is our life. . . . [A] Christian should live as Christ lived, making the affections of Christ his own, so that he can exclaim with St. Paul:* non vivo ego, vivit vero in me Christus *(Gal 2:10), it is no longer I who live, but Christ who lives in me.*[19]

Fidelity consists precisely in this: in living, wanting, and feeling in accord with Christ—not because we "disguise ourselves" as Christ, but because this becomes our own way of being. Then, in following God's will, in being faithful, we are deeply free, because we do what we want, what we like, what we "feel like" doing. Deeply free and deeply faithful. Deeply faithful and deeply happy.

19. St. Josemaría, *Christ is Passing By*, 103.

FOUR

The Most Supernatural Reason

José Ignacio Murillo

AT THE BEGINNING OF his public life, in the synagogue at Nazareth, our Lord read aloud a passage from Isaiah (61:1–2):

> The Spirit of the Lord is upon me, because he has anointed me to bring the good news to the poor. He has sent me to proclaim release to prisoners and recovery of sight to the blind, to let the oppressed

> go free, and to proclaim the year of the Lord's favor. (Lk 4:18–19, NCB)

And rolling up the scroll he declared: "Today this scripture has been fulfilled in your hearing" (Lk 4:21).

The first Christians had a deep, joyful awareness of freedom. For them, Jesus was the Savior. He had not freed them from one yoke just to lay another one on them. He had broken the shackles that prevented them from living life to the full. This new and fuller life was now reflected in the joy that overflowed in their lives. "Rejoice always," exhorts St. Paul, "pray constantly, give thanks in all circumstances, for this is the will of God in Christ Jesus for you" (1 Thes 5:16–18).

In the beginning God created man as lord of all creation. In the words of St. Gregory of Nyssa,

> The best Artificer made our nature as it were a formation fit for the exercise of royalty, preparing it at once by superior advantages of soul, and by the very form of the body, to be such as to be adapted for royalty: for the soul immediately shows its royal and exalted character . . . in that it owns no lord, and is self-governed, swayed autocratically by its own will; for to whom else does this belong than to a king?[1]

1. Gregory of Nyssa, "On the Making of Man," 4.

Through sin man was reduced to slavery, but God raised him up with the hope of future salvation (see Gen 3:15). This desire to redeem us was shown, for example, when he freed his people from the slavery of Egypt and promised them a land which, although they would have to fight for it, would be the Promised Land, God's gift, where they could worship him in freedom.

God stakes everything on our freedom. The first commandment, on which, Christ says, the Law and the prophets depend, is the law of love: love for God above all things and for one's neighbor as oneself (see Mt 22:37-40). This is no ordinary law. Other things can be commanded, imposed through force and coercion. But not love. God asks for it, as a lover, only after showing his great love for his people, his care and affection made clear in so many ways. True love can only be invited, after showing that we are worthy of it, since it can only be the fruit of freedom. And to discover and let ourselves be caught up by this love, it is essential to "foster interior freedom, which leads us to do things for love."[2]

The Meaning of Freedom

God has created us free precisely so that we may truly love him. This is how he looks on us and delights in us. We

2. Fernando Ocáriz, Pastoral Letter, February 14, 2017, no. 8.

find this hard to understand because we human beings are unable to create free beings. At the most we can produce robots that perform the tasks for which we designed them, or we imitate freedom by creating artifacts that operate in a random fashion. But we are incapable of producing something that can decide for itself. That is what God does in creating us and redeeming us from the sin that limited our freedom.

To be free is not primarily to be unrestrained by external conditions but rather to be capable of answering for our actions and responses. Thus, freedom goes hand in hand with responsibility. To be free is to be capable of taking responsibility, and to be answerable for our actions to other people and first to our Creator.

Freedom, then, is not something added on, a feature that we could dispense with and still be ourselves. The freedom that God wants for us is real freedom, rooted in the depths of our being. To recognize this is a great step forward for mankind's progress.

> An ardent desire for freedom, the demand for it on the part of persons and peoples is a positive sign of our times. Acknowledging the freedom of each woman and man means acknowledging that they are persons; masters of their own acts and responsible for them, able to direct their own lives.[3]

3. Fernando Ocáriz, Pastoral Letter, January 9, 2018, no. 1.

God, who loves us as we are because he has created us, wants us to be free because he loves us for ourselves and he can only be satisfied when we freely and lovingly open our heart to him: "My son, give me your heart" (Prov 23:26). Thus, we can understand why St. Josemaría said that *because I really want to*[4] is the most supernatural reason for doing what is good. It is supernatural because it combines the mystery of God's creative and redemptive love with the genuine response of his beloved creature: recognizing God as our Father and trustingly accepting his Will, since he only wants what is good for his children.

God has placed our destiny in our own hands. Not in the sense that by our own efforts we can attain what he has prepared for us, but that we have the power to turn freely to him, who is the One who can make us happy.[5] Realizing that we have the capacity to give our love freely to God can at first frighten us. Nevertheless, if we truly decide that we want to say yes to him, the conviction that we are free fills us with joy and hope. As God's children, we feel secure in the measure to which we rely on him. Hence, we understand why St. Josemaría, reflecting on his own vocation, exclaimed: *Doesn't it make you very happy to see that fidelity*

---

4. St. Josemaría, *Christ is Passing By*, 17.

5. "But [nature] did give man free-will, with which he can turn to God, that God may make him happy. 'For what we do by means of our friends, is done, in a sense, by ourselves'." St. Thomas Aquinas, *Summa Theologiae* I–II, q. 5 a. 5 ad 1.

depends to a great extent on us? I am excited at the thought that God loves me and has wanted his Work to depend on my response as well. And it makes me happy to be able to tell Him, freely, "Lord, I love you too; count on my littleness."[6]

Reflecting on our freedom helps us to base our life on the reality that we are God's children. We are not mass-produced, identical units: our response is unique because we are each loved by God with a special love. But we can lose the awareness of our freedom if we fail to use it. Then we will naturally feel more and more constricted, conditioned, and even coerced by our moods or surroundings. We may begin to doubt if we really are free and even if freedom is worthwhile or makes any sense.

Nevertheless, we Christians know that freedom does have a meaning. It is not just that we are free from bonds, with the power to make our own decisions. There is not much point in setting someone free and telling them they can go wherever they want, if there is nowhere for them to go or if they have no idea how to get there. But God not only grants us the ability to throw off what limits and imprisons us; he also opens to us an unlimited horizon to fulfill our deepest desires. For the One who created our freedom in no way limits its unfolding. He opens to us the possibility of limitless growth, for this is how we free creatures imitate

6. St. Josemaría, *Alone with God*, 324.

God. And he offers us, in union with his Only Begotten Son, the possibility of developing our personality to the full.

True Freedom

St. Josemaría saw his work as

> *aimed at helping each person to face up to all the demands of their life and to discover what God wants from them in particular—without in any way limiting that holy independence and blessed responsibility which are the features of a Christian conscience. This way of acting and this spirit are based on respect for the transcendence of revealed truth and love for the freedom of the human person. They are also based on a realization that history is undetermined and open to a variety of human options—all of which God respects.*[7]

The only attitude that accords with the dignity of God's children is to feel as *free as the birds*[8] to do what we truly want, even when, like Christ, what we want requires humiliation and self-surrender for love. It is not just a matter of acting as if we were free. If we really want to follow Jesus, we must search within ourselves for the source of

7. St. Josemaría, *Christ is Passing By*, 99.
8. St. Josemaría, Letter 14 September 1951, 38.

true freedom—the reality that we are God's children—and act accordingly. Then we will attain the freedom of spirit that "is the capacity and habitual attitude to act out of love, especially in the effort to follow what God is asking of us in each circumstance."[9]

Taking our freedom seriously leads to spontaneity and initiative. In contrast, the lack of freedom is often revealed by a tendency to act out of fear. Theologians give the name "servile fear" to the fear of punishment that can stop people from sinning. This fear can be the start of a return to God, but Christian life cannot be built only on servile fear. For "there is no fear in love, but perfect love casts out fear" (1 Jn 4:18), and we must "act as those who are to be judged under the law of liberty" (Jas 2:12).

Fear can appear in many areas of our life. People who are afraid, even though they want the good, are really driven by the evil they seek to escape. So, when fear is the driving force of our actions, we easily turn in on ourselves and get confused, to the point of losing sight of the true motives for our actions and the good things we want to achieve. But if we love God, if we truly want to love him, he will free us from fear, because for those who love God everything works together for the good (see Rom 8:28). This conviction drives

9. Fernando Ocáriz, Pastoral Letter, January 9, 2018, no. 5.

away our needless fears and enables us to enjoy the full freedom of God's children, acting cheerfully and responsibly.

It is true that we do not say yes to God once and for all. We are creatures whose lives unfold in time, and we have to renew and strengthen our response over time. Moreover, since we are called to respond freely, our Lord wants from us a progressively more genuine response. Sometimes he even seems to hide his face from us, so that our loyalty to him will become ever freer and fuller. He wants to purify us from external and secondary motives, so that we act not out of fear but out of love. He is inviting us to a more genuine fidelity, which is not merely a matter of preserving something already achieved, but rather of joyfully renewing, in the most varied circumstances, our generous self-giving to God.

It is good to remind ourselves often that we are not machines, nor animals living merely by instincts, but free beings. Our future is completely open and depends on our own initiative. Thus, we are helped to escape anonymity and to live facing God and other people with a free and personal response, accompanied by a sense of responsibility. Then we will be able to open a genuine dialogue with God, in a personal relationship that gives rise to a true and deep friendship. And the fruit of our friendship with God will be the burning desire to bring God's love and the accompanying sense of freedom to everyone.

Our friendship with others will be a great help here:

> Friendship is itself apostolate; friendship is itself a dialogue in which we give and receive light. In friendship plans are forged and we mutually open new horizons. In friendship we rejoice in what is good and support one another in what is difficult; we have a good time with one another, since God wants us to be happy.[10]

10. Fernando Ocáriz, Pastoral Letter, January 9, 2018, no. 14.

FIVE

Gratitude Spurs Us to Struggle

Justin Gillespie

"FOR IT WILL BE as when a man going on a journey called his servants and entrusted to them his property; to one he gave five talents, to another two, to another one, to each according to his ability. Then he went away" (Mt 25:14–15). We know Jesus' story about the talents very well and, as with all Scripture, it never ceases to invite us to a better understanding of our relationship with God.

Jesus' parable tells of a man who generously entrusts a large part of his wealth to three of his servants. By doing so he is treating them not as mere servants but rather as coworkers in his business. Hence "entrust" is precisely the right word here. He doesn't give detailed instructions, telling them exactly what to do. He leaves it in their hands.

Judging by their reactions—the effort they put into multiplying their master's capital—two of them immediately understand him. They appreciate their master's gesture as a sign of confidence in them. We could even say that they see it as a sign of love; and so they seek to thank him by responding with love, even though he didn't make any further demands or set conditions. "He who had received the five talents went at once and traded with them; and he made five talents more" (Mt 25:16). Similarly, the one who had received the two talents made two talents more.

The third servant, however, perceives something very different. He feels he is being tested and so he must not fail. For him, what matters most is to avoid making a mistake, to avoid failure. "But he who had received the one talent went and dug in the ground and hid his master's money" (Mt 25:18). He is frightened by the possibility of displeasing and even angering his master, and by the consequences he imagines could follow. "Master, I knew you to be a hard man, reaping where you did not sow, and gathering where you did not winnow; so I was afraid, and I went and hid your talent in the ground. Here you have what is yours".

(Mt 25:24–25). As he believes his master is harsh and unjust, he doesn't feel that anything has been "entrusted" to him. He sees it all as a tiresome trial, not as an opportunity. And not wanting to fail in this trial, he chooses to act in the safest possible way with what belongs to someone else and coldly returns the money: "Here you have what is yours ."

These two very different reactions can help us reflect on how we ourselves respond to what God our Father has "entrusted" to us: our life, our Christian vocation. These have an immense value in his eyes, and he has placed them in our hands. How do we respond?

Struggling Out of Gratitude, Not Fear

For the first two servants, their master's confidence was a real gift. They knew that they didn't deserve it, that they had no right to expect such responsibility would be given them. In a new way, they understood that their relationship with their master was not based on the success or failure of what they did but on how their master viewed them. More than what they were at present, he could see what they could become. Hence, we can easily imagine the deep sense of gratitude that arose in their hearts. To be looked at with eyes of hope is truly a gift, and the most natural response to a gift is to want to give something in return.

If we don't keep this in mind, we can sometimes be mistaken about the role of struggle in our Christian life.

If we struggle to succeed in order to "merit" being loved, it will be very difficult to experience genuine peace. To strive to be loved, even if only subconsciously, always means that failures and reverses will lead to deep discouragement or, even worse, bitterness in our soul. But grounding our struggle on gratitude helps to avoid this problem.

The parable also suggests that the first two servants found a sense of mission in this gift—a unique, personal mission. The master, we are told, gave "to each according to his ability" (Mt 25:15). It is unlikely that the servants had any experience of investing and overseeing such enormous sums of money. But by showing trust in them, by seeing what they could become, their master was calling them to "be more," to strive to reach further. In other words, he was entrusting them with a special personal mission.

As in the parable, God our Father also calls each of us according to what he knows we can become. This is what really matters, and what we want to rediscover in our prayer: how God sees us, not how we see ourselves. We want to make sure that our struggle is centered on him, not on ourselves.

A Struggle Inspired by Jesus' Example

We all long for peace and consolation, rest from all our labors. Jesus understands this very well. "Come to me, all who labor and are heavy laden, and I will give you rest. Take my yoke upon you, and learn from me; for I am gentle and lowly in heart, and you will find rest for your souls. For my yoke is easy, and my burden is light" (Mt 11:28–30).

"If any man would come after me, let him deny himself and take up his cross and follow me" (Mk 8:34). These words of Jesus are not a severe demand, imposed arbitrarily. Rather they are a source of immense consolation. Christ goes before us and experiences in his own flesh the challenges, fears, and sufferings that come, in a world marred by sin, from freely responding to the Father's call.

St. Josemaría encouraged each of us to discover in our own lives how to be other "Simons of Cyrene" in helping Christ to carry the cross. *For a soul in love it is no misfortune to become voluntarily Christ's Simon of Cyrene and, in this way, to give such close company to his suffering humanity, reduced to a state of rags and tatters. For if we do this, we can be certain of our closeness to God, who blesses us by choosing us for this task.*[1]

We discover that our struggle is taking place *with* Jesus. It means union with him in our efforts right now, not just when we succeed. To accept the struggle freely, as one of the consequences of accepting the gift of our Christian vocation, opens the door to the discovery that Jesus himself is helping us in our struggle. And so *it is not just any cross we are carrying. We discover it is the Cross of Christ,*

1. St. Josemaría, *Friends of God*, 132.

and with it the consolation of knowing that our Redeemer has taken it upon himself to bear its weight.[2] Alongside Jesus we can look at the Cross and see not pointless and meaningless suffering, but rather victory and redemption. We come to see the meaning of the challenges and difficulties that necessarily arise when we try to follow faithfully Christ's example in carrying out the Father's will and bearing abundant fruit.

Grace Does Not Eliminate Struggle but Transforms It

Perhaps the servant who buried the talent entrusted to him felt overwhelmed, or even saddened by the efforts he saw his companions making. Comparing himself with them and feeling inadequate for such a job, he looked for an easier, safer way. So he dug a hole and buried the gift that had been entrusted to him, together with all the possibilities that came with it. The same drama is repeated every time we evade the effort and discomfort involved in pursuing anything worthwhile in life. We must never forget that the struggle and effort required by a loving search for the good are neither unjust nor arbitrary. They are intrinsic to the very nature of life in our fallen world, the life that our Lord has sanctified. On our way through life, union with Jesus

2. St. Josemaría, *Friends of God*, 132.

comes about precisely through struggle: a free, loving struggle to grow in the supernatural and human virtues. God's grace is not a substitute for the effort that is intrinsic to each person's life, but rather unites it to God himself.

Our effort and struggle are not an expression of self-sufficiency or "neo-Pelagianism." For as St. Paul wrote to the Philippians: ". . . God is at work in you, both to will and to work for his good pleasure" (Phil 2:13). The struggle, then, is not opposed to the action of grace in us. In the final analysis, growing in the theological virtues is simply a matter of growing in love, both divine and human love, and holiness *is the fullness of charity.*[3]

St. Josemaría expressed this same theological truth in these terms: *Later, while talking to our Lord in your prayer, you understood that fighting is a synonym for love, and you asked for a greater love, with no fear of the struggle awaiting you, since you would be fighting for Him, with Him and in Him.*[4] The more we try to live our struggle as a "struggle to love," the more we will want this love, this struggle to grow. We will overcome the temptation to bury the gifts we have received in order to avoid the effort required, and instead invest those gifts, taking on all the struggle this requires.

3. St. Josemaría, *Furrow*, 739.
4. St. Josemaría, *Furrow*, 158.

Free to Grow, Free to Learn

In his pastoral letter of January 9, 2018, the Prelate helps us to understand in greater depth the close relationship between freedom and struggle in our lives. "The freer we are, the more we can love. And this love is demanding. 'Love bears all things, believes all things, hopes all things, endures all things' (1 Cor 13:7)."[5] At the same time, the more we love, the freer we feel, even at difficult or disagreeable times. "The more intense our charity is, the freer we are. We also act with freedom of spirit when we don't feel like doing something or find it especially difficult, if we do it out of love, that is, not because we like it, but because we choose to."[6]

"Our faith in God's love for each one of us (see 1 Jn 4:16) leads us to respond with love. We can love because he has loved us first (see 1 Jn 4:10). It fills us with security to know that God's infinite Love is to be found not only at the origin of our existence but also at every moment in our lives. For God is closer to us than we are to ourselves."[7]

St. Josemaría said,

> *Think a moment about those of your colleagues who are outstanding for their professional prestige, their integrity, or their spirit of service and self-sacrifice. Isn't it true that they devote many hours of the day, and even of*

---

5. Fernando Ocáriz, Pastoral Letter, January 9, 2018, no. 5.
6. Fernando Ocáriz, Pastoral Letter, January 9, 2018, no. 5.
7. Fernando Ocáriz, Pastoral Letter, January 9, 2018, no. 4.

the night to their jobs? Isn't there something we can learn from them?[8]

We can undoubtedly learn to struggle better, and thus be free to love more. And what we can learn from those who struggle best is that they tend to have an "open struggle." They don't see their aptitudes and talents as fixed or determined. Like the first two servants in Jesus' parable, they understand that what has been given them is intended to grow through their effort and struggle.

As with the servants in the parable, God has entrusted us with a wonderful mission. He has chosen to count on us to make his infinite love present in the middle of our world.

Giving love to God and to others is the most proper act of freedom. "Love *fulfills* freedom, it redeems it. Love enables freedom to discover its origin and its end, in the Love of God."[9]

The two servants who cultivated their master's gift discovered a much greater reward than they could ever have imagined. "Well done, good and faithful servant; you have been faithful over a little, I will set you over much; enter into the joy of your master" (Mt 25:23). This is the joy that we seek, and it is also the joy that accompanies us in our struggle, a struggle filled with hope: "I consider that the sufferings of this present time are not worth comparing with the glory that is to be revealed to us" (Rom 8:18).

8. St. Josemaría, *Friends of God*, 60.

9. Fernando Ocáriz, Pastoral Letter, January 9, 2018, no. 4.

SIX

Beloved, Called, Sent Out: A Sense of Mission

Lucas Buch

IN THE ACTS OF the Apostles there's a scene that has never lost any of its impact. After being imprisoned, the apostles were miraculously set free by an angel. But instead of fleeing, they returned to the temple to preach. Once again, they were arrested and taken before the chief priests. Surprised to see them again, the chief priests admonished them: "We strictly charged you not to teach in this name." Undaunted, the apostles replied: "We must obey God rather than men" (Acts 5:28–29).

The first Christians inherited this deep conviction. The Book of Acts contains many examples, and the history of the first centuries of Christianity speaks for itself. Again and again, we find the same need being candidly expressed: "We cannot but speak of what we have seen and heard" (Acts 4:20). The first faithful are willing to risk being punished, and even being put to death, without losing their cheerfulness.

A Call that Continues to Resound Today

We might be tempted to think that a great gulf exists between us and the first Christians, since they possessed a degree of holiness to which we could never aspire. Their physical closeness to Christ—or at least to one of the twelve—made them little less than impeccable and filled them with a fire that nothing and nobody could extinguish. But we need only open the Gospels to realize that this wasn't the case.

The apostles often showed themselves to be people with weaknesses and failings, just as we are. For one thing, they had no special intellectual training. Jesus sent out the first seventy-two when they had spent only a few weeks with him (see Lk 10:1–12). Nevertheless, the faithful in the early Church were very clear about one thing: that our Lord Jesus

Christ had died and risen for each of them. Perhaps that is why Pope Francis reminded us, with St. Paul's words, that "the Lord has chosen each one of us to be 'holy and blameless before Him in love' (Eph 1:4–5)."[1]

In every age, the Church is aware of having received a call from Christ, and with it a task; moreover, she herself *is* that call and that task. "The Church on earth is by her very nature missionary since, according to the plan of the Father, she has her origin in the mission of the Son and the Holy Spirit."[2] This is not merely a beautiful desire or a human endeavor; rather her "mission continues and develops in the course of history the mission of Christ himself."[3]

Hence our life, too, is the response to a call; a task in the world and for the world. Our Lord has sought us out and sent us into the world to share with everyone the salvation we have received. *"Go, preach the gospel . . . I will be with you." Jesus has said this, and He has said it to you.*[4] To *me*; and to each man and each woman. In God's presence, we can each consider this reality: "I am a Christian because God has called me and has sent me forth." And, moved by

---

1. Pope Francis, Apostolic Exhortation on the Call to Holiness in Today's World *Gaudete et Exsultate* (March 19, 2018), no. 2. Vatican website: www.vatican.va.

2. Second Vatican Council, Decree on the Mission Activity of the Church *Ad Gentes* (December 7, 1965), 2.

3. Second Vatican Council, *Ad Gentes*, 5.

4. St. Josemaría, *The Way*, 904.

the strength of his Spirit, from the depths of our heart we will answer with the words of the psalm, "I delight to do thy will, O my God." (Ps 40:8).

An "Imperative Command"

During the 1950s St. Josemaría made trips to various European countries to see the first faithful of the Work who had gone there to begin the Work's apostolic activities. "The afternoon meditations he gave for those with him, often had as their theme the Lord's words to the apostles, 'I chose you and appointed you that you should go and bear fruit . . . *ut eatis*' (Jn 15:16)."[5]

We have read and listened to many stories about the first people who followed our Lord in Opus Dei: the first circle in the Porta Coeli shelter; the first residence on Ferraz Street; the intense family life St. Josemaría kept alive during the dramatic years of the Spanish Civil War; the first expansion in Spain; the arrival in Rome; the rapid spread throughout the world . . . Those young—and not so young—people followed the Founder with the awareness that they were answering a real call from God. As Pope Francis wrote: "Goodness always tends to spread. Every

5. Andrés Vázquez de Prada, *The Founder of Opus Dei: The Life of Josemaría Escrivá*, vol. 3, The Divine Ways on Earth (New York: Scepter, 2005), p. 236.

authentic experience of truth and beauty seeks by its very nature to spread to others."[6]

Some were young and enthusiastic, others quieter and more thoughtful; but they were all convinced that behind that young priest and the work he had in hand was an explicit desire of God. And so they were ready to say yes to our Lord's invitation to leave everything and follow him. They had experienced what St. Josemaría often told them: *Don't forget, my sons, that we are not just souls who have joined with other souls to do a good thing. That is a lot . . . and yet it is little. We are apostles who are fulfilling an imperative command of Christ.*[7] And since they followed Jesus with complete freedom, that command was not burdensome but just the opposite. As St. Josemaría also said: *This supernatural conviction of the divine nature of the enterprise will give you such intense enthusiasm and love for the Work that you will feel overjoyed to sacrifice yourselves to bring it to fulfillment.*[8] They did not need anyone to explain the meaning of these words: they lived it in their own lives.

---

6. Pope Francis, *Evangelii Gaudium*, 9.

7. St. Josemaría, Instruction, March 19, 1934, no. 27. The text is taken from the *The Way: Historical-Critical Edition*, ed. Pedro Rodríguez (New York: Scepter, 2009), commentary on point 942.

8. St. Josemaría, Instruction, 19 March 1934, no. 49. Quoted in Vázquez de Prada, *The Founder of Opus Dei: The Life of Josemaría Escrivá*, vol. 1, The Early Years (New York: Scepter, 2001), p. 444.

We Don't "Do Apostolate," We Are Apostles!

These stories about the first people in the Work are moving to recall. Many centuries have gone by since the preaching of the apostles. Not even a hundred years have gone by since the founding of the Work. The whole history of the Church shows us that our Lord's call continues to resound down through the centuries in the heart of each believer—and in our own. Christ, with his love, has entered our life (see Phil 3:12). Each of us is called to embrace his love and allow him to transform our lives. The more our life is centered on Christ, the more the "sense of mission that our vocation entails will be strengthened, along with our complete and joyful self-giving."[9]

Like the first Christians, the first people in the Work found Christ, and wholeheartedly embraced his love and the mission it entailed. And they saw how their lives were marvelously transformed. We see fulfilled in them what the Prelate reminded us of shortly after his election:

> We are free in order to love God who calls, God who is love and puts love into us so that we can love Him and love others. This charity makes us fully aware of our mission, which is "not an apostolate exercised

9. Fernando Ocáriz, Pastoral Letter, February 14, 2017, no. 8.

sporadically or occasionally, but habitually and by vocation, adopted as the ideal of our whole life."[10]

The apostolic mission that fills our entire life is not a task that someone has imposed on us, nor a job we must add to our other daily duties. It is the exact expression of our very identity, as revealed to us by our vocation: "We do not 'do apostolate,' we are apostles!"[11] At the same time, by living out this mission, we strengthen our identity as apostles. Here the life of St. Paul is always a source of inspiration. When we read the story of his journeys, it is striking how often his mission does not achieve the expected result. On his first journey, for example, he is rejected by the Jews in Pisidian Antioch, and afterwards thrown out of the city; he must flee from Iconium under threat of death (see Acts 13–14).

Nevertheless, the apostle to the Gentiles never loses sight of the call Jesus had addressed to him on the way to Damascus, and later confirmed in that city. Hence, he never tires of repeating, "The love of Christ urges us on" (2 Cor 5:14, NRSVCE). Even when writing to people he has not yet met, he does not fear to introduce himself as "Paul, a servant of Jesus Christ, called to be an apostle, set apart for the gospel of God" (Rom 1:1). That is who he is: "called

10. Fernando Ocáriz, Pastoral Letter, February 14, 2017, no. 9.
11. Fernando Ocáriz, Pastoral Letter, February 14, 2017, no. 9.

to be an apostle," an apostle by vocation. And he addresses that community of faithful as people "called to belong to Jesus Christ . . . God's beloved in Rome, who are called to be saints" (Rom1:6–7). Paul knows that he has been called by God, but he is equally aware that so have all the faithful.[12] His sense of mission leads him to live a fraternity that goes beyond earthly ties.

Similarly, to the question "Who am I?" we can each reply, "I am someone loved by God, saved by Jesus Christ, chosen to be an apostle, called to bring the love I've received to many people. So apostolate isn't a job that I have, it's a necessity for me." When we truly find Christ, we realize that we are meant to be salt and light, and therefore need to give savor and provide illumination wherever we may be. This is a discovery that "revolutionizes" our spiritual life and that no one else can make for us.

With the Strength of the Holy Spirit

When we discover our Lord in our life, when we realize that we are loved, called, chosen, and we decide to follow him,

---

12. This is in fact the origin of the Greek word *ekklesia* (in Latin *ecclesia*), meaning "church," which literally means "those called together," that is, "all of us who have been baptized and believe in God, called by Our Lord." *Compendium of the Catechism of the Catholic Church* (Washington, DC: Libreria Editrice Vaticana—United States Conference of Catholic Bishops, 2006), 121. See *Catechism of the Catholic Church*, 751, for the parallel derivation of the English word *church*.

it is as though a new light is lit within us; it is a mysterious impulse that spurs a person to dedicate their noblest energies to an activity that, over time, becomes a way of life.[13]

The apostolic mission means, first, that "a new light has been lit within us." The darkness, the uncertainty about the meaning of life, vanishes. The invitation Christ addresses to us enables us to understand our past and offers us a clear route for the future.

The light of this mission is at the same time an "impulse" impelling us on. But it is not a human force. Of course, there will be times when we feel enthusiastic, when we feel a burning desire to enkindle those around us with Christ's fire. But everyone who has been following our Lord for any length of time has experienced that the human impulse comes and goes. This is part of being human, as the saints too have experienced. The life of Bl. Álvaro del Portillo, to go no further, reminds us of this reality. As we know, soon after joining the Work he had to write to the Founder telling him that his enthusiasm had disappeared.[14]

So we should never lose sight of the fact that our true strength, the dynamism that spurs us to get out of ourselves to serve others, "is not a strategy, but the actual strength of the Holy Spirit, uncreated Charity."[15] Indeed, no motiva-

---

13. St. Josemaría, Letter, January 9, 1932, no. 9.

14. See *The Way: Historical-Critical Edition*, commentary on no. 994.

15. Fernando Ocáriz, Pastoral Letter, February 14, 2017, no. 9.

tion "will be enough, unless the fire of the Holy Spirit burns in our hearts." Therefore, "keeping our missionary fervor alive calls for firm trust in the Holy Spirit, for it is He who 'helps us in our weakness' (Rom 8:26). But this generous trust must be nourished, and so we need to invoke the Spirit constantly."[16] The faithful of the Work invoke him daily in the Holy Mass, and in vocal prayers such as the Rosary and the *Preces* of the Work.

Sometimes we may find it helpful to address him with some special prayer, for example the Pentecost Sequence *Veni Sancte Spiritus* ("Holy Spirit, Lord of Light"), the hymn *Veni Creator Spiritus* ("Come Holy Spirit, Creator, Come"), or one of the many other prayers to him that have been composed down through the centuries. In all of them we ask him to come, to transform us, to fill us with the love and strength that imbued our Lord's actions. We ask him: "Spirit of love, Creator and Sanctifier of souls, your first work in us is to transform us so that we resemble Jesus. Help me, Spirit of Love, to adapt myself to the pattern of Jesus, to think like Jesus, to speak like Jesus, to suffer like Jesus, to behave like Jesus."[17]

---

16. Pope Francis, *Evangelii Gaudium*, 261, 280. In the same document he suggests: "Let us call upon Him today, firmly rooted in prayer, for without prayer all our activity risks being fruitless and our message empty" (259).

17. Alexis Riaud, *The Holy Spirit Acting in Our Souls* (Manila: Sinag-Tala, 1992), p. 34.

Thus, the transforming impulse of the Holy Spirit will give us a heart on fire like Jesus' heart, and the apostolic mission will be the very blood pumped by our heart. It will take shape in us little by little in *an activity that, over time, becomes a way of life.*[18] If we let ourselves be led by God's love, if we stay attentive to his inspirations and take notice of his small suggestions, the apostolate will become "a way of life" that configures our own identity. What matters is to stay open to the Paraclete's action, attentive to "how we can better accomplish the mission entrusted to us at our baptism,"[19] the mission that is the fulfillment of our whole life.

---

18. St. Josemaría, Letter, January 9, 1937.
19. Pope Francis, *Gaudete et Exsultate*, 174.

SEVEN

Apostles in the Middle of the World: A Sense of Mission

Lucas Buch

St. Luke gives a vivid picture of the life of the first believers in Jerusalem after Pentecost: "Day by day, attending the temple together and breaking bread in their homes, they partook of food with glad and generous hearts, praising God and having favor with all the people. And the Lord added to their number day by day those who were being saved" (Acts 2:46–47). But soon obstacles would arise: the imprisonment of John and Peter, the martyrdom of Stephen, and finally, open persecution.

In this context, the evangelist relates something quite surprising: "Now those who were scattered went about preaching the word" (Acts 8:4). It is striking that the disciples did not stop proclaiming the salvation brought by Christ, even though this entailed risking their lives. A little later, we see a similar account: "Now those who were scattered because of the persecution that arose over Stephen traveled as far as Phoeni'cia and Cyprus and Antioch, speaking the word to none except Jews" (Acts 11:19). What moved those first faithful to speak about Christ, even while fleeing from persecution? It was the joy that filled their hearts: "We declare to you what we have seen and heard so that you also may have fellowship with us" (1 Jn 1:3, NRSVCE). They announce it, quite simply, so "that our joy may be complete" (1 Jn 1:4). The love they had discovered had to be shared; their joy was contagious. Shouldn't we Christians do likewise today?

The Way of Friendship

A small feature in this scene from the Acts is quite significant. Among those who had been scattered "were some of them, men of Cyprus and Cyre'ne, who on coming to Antioch spoke to the Greeks also, preaching the Lord Jesus"

(Acts 11:20). The Christians did not move in special circles, nor did they wait to reach suitable places to announce the life and freedom they had received. They each shared their faith quite naturally, in their immediate surroundings, with the people God placed in their midst—like Philip with the Ethiopian returning from Jerusalem, or like the married couple Aquila and Priscilla with the young man Apollos (see Acts 8:26–40; 18:24–26). The love of God that filled their hearts led them to be concerned about everyone, sharing with them the treasure "that can enlarge us and make those who receive it better and happier."[1] If our heart too is filled with God's love, we will share it with those closest to us. And we will feel impelled to reach more and more people, to share with them the new life that our Lord gives us. As it was then, now too it will be true that "the hand of the Lord was with them, and a great number became believers and turned to the Lord" (Acts 11:21, NRSVCE).

A second idea that we can consider here, in the light of history, is that the Church grew and continues to grow above all through the charity of her individual members, rather than through structured and organized action. The structure and organization would come later, as the fruit of this charity and in service of it. We have seen something similar in the history of the Work. Those who first followed St. Josemaría loved the others with sincere affection, and

1. Pope Francis, *Gaudete et Exsultate*, 131.

this provided the environment for God's message to open a path forward. We see this in the first student residence of the Work:

> Those who lived at 33 Luchana Street were friends united by the same Christian spirit that the Father transmitted. Hence a person who found himself at home in the environment created around Don Josemaría and those alongside him, came back again. Indeed, people who first came to the flat on Luchana Street by invitation, kept coming back out of friendship.[2]

It is good for us to recall these aspects of the history of the Church and the Work, given the risk that, as both have grown so much with the passing of time, we could come to rely more on existing apostolic structures than on our personal apostolic efforts. Recently the Prelate reminded us: "The current situation of evangelization makes it more necessary than ever to give priority to personal contact. This relational aspect is at the heart of the way of doing apostolate that St. Josemaría found in the Gospel narratives."[3]

This is only natural. The dynamic force at work in the apostolate is charity, which is a gift from God, and *in a Christian, in a child of God, friendship and charity are one*

---

2. José Luis González Gullón, *DYA: La Academia y Residencia en la historia del Opus Dei (1933–1939)* (Madrid: Rialp, 2016), p. 196.

3. Fernando Ocáriz, Pastoral Letter, February 14, 2017, no. 9.

and the same thing. They are a divine light which spreads warmth.[4] Friendship is love, and for a child of God it is authentic charity. Therefore, it is not that we seek friends in order to do apostolate, but rather friendship and apostolate are manifestations of the same love. Moreover,

> friendship itself is apostolate; friendship itself is a dialogue in which we give and receive light. In friendship we mutually open new horizons. We rejoice in what is good and we support one another in what is difficult; we have a good time with one another, since God wants us to be happy.[5]

We should ask ourselves: How much do I care for my friends? Do I share with them the joy that comes from knowing how much God loves us? And do I try to reach more people, people who may never have known a believer very well, in order to draw them closer to God's love?

At the Crossroads of the World

"For if I preach the gospel, that gives me no ground for boasting. For necessity is laid upon me. Woe to me if I do not preach the gospel!" (1 Cor 9:16). These words of St. Paul are a constant call to the Church. Similarly, his awareness of

---

4. St. Josemaría, *The Forge*, no. 565.
5. Fernando Ocáriz, Pastoral Letter, January 9, 2018, no. 14.

having been called by God for a mission is an ever-present example: "For if I do this of my own will, I have a reward; but if not of my own will, I am entrusted with a commission" (1 Cor 9:17). The apostle to the Gentiles was aware of having been called to bring Christ's name "before the Gentiles and kings and the sons of Israel" (Acts 9:15), and hence he felt a holy urgency to reach everyone.

On his second trip, when the Holy Spirit led him to Greece, Paul's heart expanded, and he sensed a thirst for God around him. In Athens, while waiting for those who had stayed in Berea, St. Luke tells us that "he was greatly distressed to see that the city was full of idols" (Acts 17:16). As usual, he went first to the synagogue. But the response there was half-hearted, so Paul went to the Areopagus, where the Athenians asked: "May we know what this new teaching is which you present?" (Acts 17:19). And so, in the Athenian Areopagus, where the most influential currents of contemporary thought were debated, Paul announced the name of Jesus Christ.

Like the apostle, we too "are called to contribute, with initiative and spontaneity, to improving the world and the culture of our times, so that they open themselves to God's plans for mankind: *cogitationes cordis eius*, the plans of his heart, which remain from 'generation to generation' (Ps 33:11)."[6] It is only natural that in the hearts of many

6. Fernando Ocáriz, Pastoral Letter, February 14, 2017, no. 8.

Christian faithful the desire is born to reach those places that "have a great impact on the future make-up of society."[7]

All this forms part of the mission of the lay faithful in the Church. As the Second Vatican Council taught,

> They are called there by God that by exercising their proper function and led by the spirit of the Gospel they may work for the sanctification of the world from within as a leaven. In this way they may make Christ known to others, especially by the testimony of a life resplendent in faith, hope and charity.[8]

This call, common to all the lay faithful, is specified in a particular way in those of us who have received the vocation to Opus Dei. St. Josemaría described the apostolate of his daughters and sons as *an intravenous injection in the bloodstream of society.*[9] He envisioned them as being zealous to bring Christ to every sector of human work: *the factory, the laboratory, the farm, the trades, the streets of the big cities and the trails of the mountains.*[10] Through their work, the laity strive to put Christ *at the center of all earthly activities.*[11]

---

7. Fernando Ocáriz, Pastoral Letter, February 14, 2017, no. 29.

8. Second Vatican Council, Dogmatic Constitution on the Church *Lumen Gentium* (November 21, 1964), 31. Vatican website: www.vatican.va.

9. St. Josemaría, Instruction, March 19, 1934, no. 42.

10. St. Josemaría, *Christ is Passing By*, 105.

11. St. Josemaría, *Christ is Passing By*, 183.

With the desire to strengthen this essential feature of the Work, Msgr. Ocáriz encouraged us, in his first letter as Prelate,

> to foster in everyone a great professional eagerness: in those who are still students and who should harbor great desires to build up society, and in those who are carrying out a profession. With a right intention, they should foster the holy ambition of going far in their profession and of making an impact.[12]

This does not mean mindlessly following the latest fashions. Rather, the faithful of Opus Dei should strive *to be up to date with modern developments and to understand the world. Together with their fellow citizens, who are their equals, they are part of the contemporary world and make it modern.*[13]

This is a beautiful task that requires from us a constant effort to get out of our small world and raise our eyes to the immense horizons of the work of salvation. The whole world awaits the vivifying presence of true Christians! Nevertheless,

> How often we are tempted to keep close to the shore! Yet the Lord calls us to put out into the deep and let down our nets (see Lk 5:4). He bids us spend our lives

---

12. Fernando Ocáriz, Pastoral Letter, February 14, 2017, no. 8.
13. *ConversationsSt.*, 26.

in his service. Clinging to him, we are inspired to put all our charisms at the service of others. May we always feel compelled by his love (see 2 Cor 5:14) and say with St. Paul: 'Woe to me if I do not preach the Gospel!' (1 Cor 9:16).[14]

Availability to Do the Work

Along with the desire to bring salvation to many people, the heart of the apostle is vigilant for all the churches (see 2 Cor 11:28). The Church has had many needs right from the very beginning. The Acts of the Apostles, for instance, tells how Barnabas sold his field and placed the proceeds at the apostles' feet (see Acts 4:37). In many of his letters St. Paul mentions the collection he was taking up for the Christians at Jerusalem. The Work is no exception here either. Just a week after arriving in Rome, on June 30, 1946, St. Josemaría wrote to the members of the General Council, then located in Madrid: *I am planning to go to Madrid as soon as possible and then return to Rome. Ricardo! We urgently need six hundred thousand pesetas. Considering our financial problems, that seems like sheer madness. But it is imperative that we get a house here.*[15] The need for buildings

14. Pope Francis, *Gaudete et Exsultate*, 130.

15. Vázquez de Prada, *The Founder of Opus Dei*, vol. 3, p. 35. As General Administrator, Ricardo Fernandez Vallespín was in charge of the financial needs of the Work.

in Rome had only just begun and, like the first Christians, everyone in the Work considered these material needs as something very personal. In more recent years, Don Javier spoke about the first two priests who went to Uruguay to begin the apostolic work of Opus Dei here. After some time in the country, they received a large donation that would have been a great help to solve their own financial problems. Nevertheless, without any hesitation, they sent all of it to Rome for the centers there.

The material needs of the Work never ceased during St. Josemaría's lifetime, and they will always be a reality. The apostolates are multiplying all over the world—thanks be to God—and the need to maintain those that already exist is a constant concern. Therefore, we need to keep alive our sense of responsibility to meet these many needs. As the Prelate reminds us, "Our love for the Church will spur us to obtain resources for the development of the apostolates."[16]

The same thing could be said about another marvelous expression of our faith in the divine origin of the call to do *opus dei* on earth. We know how joyful St. Josemaría was at seeing the cheerful self-giving of his daughters and sons. In one of his last letters, he thanked God for their *complete availability—within the duties of their personal situation in the world—to serve God in the Work.*[17] That period of uncer-

16. Fernando Ocáriz, Pastoral Letter, February 14, 2017, no. 8.
17. St. Josemaría, Letter, February 14, 1974, no. 5.

tainty and confrontation in the Church and in the world made their generous self-giving shine forth with a very special light.

> *Young people and those not so young have gone from one place to another with the greatest naturalness or have persevered faithfully in the same spot without growing tired. When needed they have completely changed their work, leaving behind what they were doing and undertaking a different task of greater apostolic interest. They have learned how to do new things. They have joyfully consented to hide and disappear, letting others move past them: going up and coming down.*[18]

Although the principal apostolic work of Opus Dei is the personal apostolate of each of its faithful,[19] we should not forget that in addition, the Work corporately supports specific social, educational, and charitable activities. These are all manifestations of the same ardent love that God has placed in our hearts. In addition, the formation given by the Work *requires a certain structure,*[20] minimal yet essential. The same sense of mission that spurs us to get close to many people, and to strive to be leaven wherever important decisions affecting the welfare of humanity are made, leads us to harbor a healthy concern for these needs of the Work.

18. St. Josemaría, Letter, February 14, 1974, no. 5.
19. See *ConversationsSt.*, 51.
20. See *ConversationsSt.*, 63.

Many faithful of Opus Dei, celibate as well as married, work in a wide variety of apostolic activities. Some take care of tasks of formation and government in the Work. Although this kind of work is not the essence of their vocation, it is a specific way of being Opus Dei. That is why the Prelate encourages the celibate members of the Work "to have an active and generous availability, when necessary, to dedicate themselves with that same professional eagerness to tasks of formation and government."[21] People do not accept those roles as an imposed assignment, which has little to do to with their own life. On the contrary, they accept them out of an awareness of having been called by God for a great mission and, like St. Paul, wanting to be "a slave to all so as to win over as many as possible" (1 Cor 9:19, NABRE). These internal tasks are, in fact, a *professional job, which demands specific and careful training.*[22] Hence when people accept jobs of this type, they should receive them with a *sense of mission*, with the desire to add their own "grain of sand" to the immense task. For the same reason, these jobs should not separate anyone from the world, but rather are the specific way for them to remain in the middle of the world, reconciling it with God. And then that work will become the "hinge" of their sanctification.

---

21. Fernando Ocáriz, Pastoral Letter, February 14, 2017, no. 8.
22. St. Josemaría, Letter, September 29, 1957, no. 9.

In the early Church, the disciples had "one heart and soul" (Acts 4:32). They loved one another truly, and lived in marvelous fraternity: "Who is weak, and I am not weak? Who is made to fall, and I am not indignant?" (2 Cor 11:29). From the place where they had first encountered the joy of the Gospel, they filled the world with light. All of them felt the urgent need to bring Christ's salvation to as many people as possible. All wanted to collaborate in the work of the apostles: by their own life of dedication, their hospitality, their material assistance, or by placing themselves at their service, like the people who accompanied St. Paul on his journeys. This is not just an image of the past but a wonderful reality today, which we see embodied in the Church and in the Work. And all of us are called to embody it in our own lives, through our free and ever-renewed response to God's gift.

EIGHT

Pleasing God

Diego Zalbidea

DURING THE SPANISH CIVIL WAR, after several months spent hiding in various places, St. Josemaría decided to leave Madrid. He had to reach a place where his life was not in constant danger, where he could begin carrying out again his apostolic mission. With a group of his spiritual sons, he crossed the Pyrenees on a dangerous journey and managed to reach Andorra. After passing through Lourdes, he made his way to Pamplona, where the bishop welcomed him and offered him lodging. There, shortly after arriving, during Christmastime 1937, he made a retreat alone. Struggling to pray, he wrote:

> *Meditation: a lot of coldness. At first, the only clear sensation was the childish desire "to make my Father-God happy when he has to judge me." Then, a strong jolt: "Jesus, say something to me!" repeated many times, full of sorrow for my inner coldness. And an invocation to my Mother in heaven, "Mama!" And to the guardian angels, and to my children who are already enjoying God. And then, lots of tears and crying . . . and prayer. Resolutions: "to be faithful to the schedule, in ordinary life."*[1]

In intimate notes, he ardently records his deep feelings and affections, the state of his soul: coldness, tears, and burning desires. He seeks refuge in his loves: God the Father, Jesus, Mary. And surprisingly, amid the great external tribulation that he was going though at that time, he made a resolution that might seem insignificant: to be faithful to the schedule, in ordinary life. This is undoubtedly one of St. Josemaría's great qualities: combining a deep and ardent relationship with God with fidelity in the daily struggle in ordinary things that might seem insignificant.

1. *The Way: Critical-Historical Edition*, commentary on no. 746, p. 880.

A Risk for Those Who Want to Please God

Pleasing someone is the opposite of saddening him, disappointing him. Since we want to love God and please him, it's only natural that we are afraid of disappointing him. But fear can sometimes stir up in our mind and heart exactly what we are trying to avoid. Moreover, fear is a negative feeling, which can't be the basis for a fulfilled life. Maybe that is why "in the Sacred Scriptures the expression 'do not be afraid' is repeated 365 times with different variations, as if to tell us that the Lord wants us to be free from fear, every day of the year."[2]

In his first pastoral letter, Mgsr. Ocáriz warned us of a certain type of fear. He encouraged us to "express the ideal of Christian life without confusing it with perfectionism and teach people how to live with and accept their own weakness and that of others; practicing, with all its consequences, a daily attitude of hopeful abandonment to God's will, grounded on divine filiation."[3] A holy person is afraid of offending God and not responding fully to his love. The perfectionist, in contrast, is afraid of not doing things well enough, and therefore of God becoming angry. Sanctity is not the same as perfectionism, although sometimes we can confuse them.

---

2. Pope Francis, *Message for the 33rd World Youth Day* (March 25, 2018). Vatican website: www.vatican.va.

3. Fernando Ocáriz, Pastoral Letter, February 14, 2017, no. 8.

How often we become angry on seeing that we have let ourselves be carried away once again by our passions, that we have sinned again, that we are weak in fulfilling the simplest resolutions. We get angry and think that God must be disappointed; we lose hope that he still loves us, that we can truly share in his life. Sadness sinks into our heart. On these occasions, we need to remember that sadness is an ally of the enemy and doesn't bring us closer to God but rather distances us from him.

When we read Christ's words in the Gospel, "Be perfect" (Mt 5:48), we want to follow this advice, to ground our life on it, but we run the risk of understanding it as, "Do everything perfectly." We can even think that, if we don't do everything with perfection, we fail to please God; we are not true disciples. But Jesus immediately clarifies the meaning of his words: "Be perfect, as your heavenly Father is perfect" (Mt 5:48). It is about the perfection that God offers us by making us sharers in his divine nature: the perfection of eternal Love, of the greatest Love, of "the Love that moves the sun and the other stars,"[4] the same Love that has created us as free beings and has saved us "while we were yet sinners" (Rom 5:8). For us, being perfect means living as God's children, aware of the value we have in his eyes, without ever losing the hope and joy that stems from sensing we are children of such a good Father.

---

4. Dante Alighieri, *The Divine Comedy: Paradiso*, canto 33.

Faced with the danger of perfectionism, we should remember that pleasing God doesn't lie in our hands, but in his. "In this is love, not that we loved God but that he loved us" (1 Jn 4:10). In fact, he has shown us his love, and therefore the first thing he expects from us is that we let him love us, in his own way.

God Loves Us Freely

Why is it so hard for us to understand God's logic? Don't we have abundant examples of how far God the Father is willing to go to make us happy? Didn't Jesus gird himself with a towel and wash the apostles' feet?

As St. Paul wrote, God did not spare his own Son in order to make it possible for us to enjoy happiness forever (see Rom 8:32). He wanted to love us with the greatest possible love, to the ultimate extreme. However, we can still sometimes think that God will only love us if we "live up to it" or "measure up." It is certainly paradoxical. Does a young child need to become "worthy" of its parents' love?

But all we must do is look at God, who is our Father, and rest in his love. In the baptism of Jesus and in his transfiguration, the voice of God the Father tells us that he is pleased with his Son. We too have been baptized and, through his passion, we share intimately in his life, his merits, his grace. As a result, God the Father can look at us pleased, delighted. The Eucharist transmits to us, among other things, a very clear message about God's feelings for us: his hunger to be close to each of us, his readiness to wait for us for as long as necessary, his yearning for intimacy and for a love that responds to his own love for us.

The Struggle of a Soul in Love

Discovering the love God has for us is the greatest motive we could find for loving. Similarly, "the primary reason for evangelizing is the love of Jesus which we have received, the experience of salvation which urges us to ever greater love of him."[5]

These are not abstract ideas. We see this in such human examples as the demoniac at Gerasa, who after being freed by Jesus and seeing his fellow citizens reject the Master "begged him that he might be with him" (Mk 5:18). We see it also in Bartimaeus, who after being cured of his blindness, "followed him on the way" (Mk 10:52). We see it finally in Peter, who only after discovering the depth of Jesus' love, his forgiveness, and trust after betraying him, can follow his call: "Follow me" (Jn 21:19). The discovery of God's love is the most powerful motive for our Christian life. That is where our struggle stems from.

St. Josemaría encouraged us to consider this from the perspective of our divine filiation:

5. Pope Francis, *Evangelii Gaudium*, 264.

> *Children . . . How they seek to behave worthily in the presence of their parents. And the children of kings, in the presence of their father the king, how they seek to uphold the royal dignity! And you? Don't you realize that you are always in the presence of the great King, your Father-God?*[6]

God's presence doesn't fill his children with fear. Not even when they fall. He himself has wanted to tell us in the clearest possible way that, even when we fall, he is waiting for us. Like the father in the parable, he is eager to come to meet us as soon as we let him, and to give us a hug and cover us with kisses (see Lk 15:20).

Faced with the possible fear of saddening God, we can ask ourselves: Does this fear unite me with God, and make me think more about him; or does it focus my attention on myself—on my expectations, on my struggle, on my achievements? Does it lead me to ask God for forgiveness in confession, and to be filled with joy when I know that he forgives me; or does it lead me to lose hope? Does it help me to start over joyfully; or does it shut me in my sadness, in my feelings of helplessness, in the frustration that is born of a struggle based on my own strength . . . and on the results that I "achieve"?

---

6. St. Josemaría, *The Way,* 265.

Mary's Smile

An event in St. Josemaría's life can help us understand this better. It is one of the notes about his interior life that he wrote down to make the task of his spiritual director easier. Although it is a bit long, it is worth quoting it entirely:

> *As always happens when I've asked this with humility, regardless of what time I've gone to bed, this morning I woke out of a deep sleep, as if I had been called, totally sure it was time for me to get up. And sure enough, it was a quarter to six. Last night, also as usual, I had asked the Lord to give me strength to overcome my laziness at wake-up time, because (I confess this to my shame) something so small is enormously hard for me and there are plenty of days when, despite that supernatural call, I stay in bed a while longer. Today, when I saw what time it was, I prayed, I struggled . . . and I stayed in bed. Finally, at six-fifteen according to my alarm clock (which has been broken for some time), I got up. Full of humiliation, I prostrated myself on the floor, acknowledging my fault, and then—with a Serviam! ["I will serve!"]—got dressed and started my meditation. And then, somewhere between six-thirty and a quarter to seven, I saw, for quite some time, that the face of my Lady of the Kisses was filled with happiness, with joy. I looked very carefully. I believed she was smiling, because it had that effect on me, even though her*

> *lips hadn't moved. Very calmly, I said to my Mother a lot of sweet things.*[7]

His effort to fulfill his resolution has perhaps been a struggle for us too at times: getting up punctually. And he failed in it. It was something that humiliated him. Nevertheless, he doesn't confuse his anger and humiliation with the magnanimity of God's heart. And he saw Our Lady smile at him, after this failure. Isn't it true that we tend to think that God is happy with us when—and at times, only when—we do things well? Why do we mistake our personal satisfaction with the smile of God, with his tenderness and affection? Do we react in the same way when we get up once again after another fall?

We have often asked Our Lady to speak well of us to our Lord—*ut loquaris pro nobis bona*. Sometimes we may even have tried to imagine those conversations between Mary and her Son. In our prayer, we can enter that intimacy and try to contemplate the love of Mary and of Jesus for each one of us.

> To seek Mary's smile is not an act of devotional or outmoded sentimentality, but rather the proper expression of the living and profoundly human relationship which binds us to her whom Christ gave us

7. Vázquez de Prada, *The Founder of Opus Dei,* vol 1, p. 361.

> as our Mother. To wish to contemplate our Lady's smile does not mean letting oneself be led by an uncontrolled imagination.[8]

Benedict XVI spoke these words in Lourdes, about the young Bernadette. In Mary's first appearance, before presenting herself as the Immaculate Conception, Our Lady simply smiled at her. "Mary first showed Bernadette her smile, as if it were the most appropriate entrance way to the revelation of her mystery."[9]

We too want to see this smile and live in its joy. Our mistakes—no matter how bad—can never erase it. If we get up once again, we can seek Mary's look and be enkindled anew with her joy.

---

8. Pope Benedict XVI, Homily, Eucharistic Celebration for the Sick (September 15, 2008). Vatican website: www.vatican.va.

9. Pope Benedict XVI, Homily, Eucharistic Celebration for the Sick.